Dokken

Into the Fire

And Other Embers Of '80s Metal History

By James Curl

Other books by James Curl
Ronnie James Dio
A Biography of a Heavy Metal Icon

JCPublications

Sacramento, Ca

Dokken

Into the Fire

And Other Embers Of '80s Metal History

By James Curl

(ISBN-13): 978-0-578-66949-6

Cover design by Chris Akin

Cover photo by Mark Weiss

Every effort was made to locate copyright information for all photographs. For any copyright infringement issues please contact James Curl at curl88@hotmail.com

<u>Acknowledgments</u>

I would like to thank the following people for their help with this book: Don Dokken, Jeff Pilson, Michael Wagener, Gary Link, Greg Leon, Kirt Dudley, Tom Werman, Wendell Neeley, Chris Akin, Michael White, Jack Russell, Peter Baltas, Reb Beach, Martin Popoff, Rob Easterday, Jon Levin, Steven R. Barry.

Table of Contents

Acknowledgements:... iii
Table of Contents:... iv
Introduction:... 1
Foreword:... 5

Chapter 1: The Sunset Strip... 14

Chapter 2: Beginnings... 21

Chapter 3: George and Mick... 38

Chapter 4: Breaking the Chains and Jeff Pilson... 50

Chapter 5: Tooth and Nail... 67

Chapter 6: The Flyer Wars and Hear 'n Aid... 81

Chapter 7: Under Lock and Key... 92

Photos: 108-130

Chapter 8: Back for the Attack and Freddy Krueger... 131

Chapter 9: The Break Up... 142

Chapter 10: Up from the Ashes and Lynch Mob... 153

Chapter 11: Dysfunctional and Shadowlife... 168

Chapter 12: Erase the Slate and the Departure of Jeff... 181

Chapter 13: Into the 2000s and John Levin... 194

Chapter 14: Lightning Strikes Again and Broken Bones... 202

Chapter 15: The Big Reunion... 218

<u>Introduction</u>

It was 1985 and I was 15 years old the first time I ever heard of Dokken. I can still vividly remember the day; a memory that is as fresh now as it was 35 years ago.

I had ridden my Torker BMX bicycle over to my friend Scott Leatherberry's house to hang out and get ready for a day at the jumps down on 13th Street. I found Scott in his room busily working on his bike.

Being the '80s, just about every kid born into Generation X was into Free Style or BMX and our bikes were basically our cars. Like most teenage boys the walls in Scott's room were covered with large posters. Several of these posters, emblazoned with words like "radical" and "awesome," were action shots of pro BMX'ers and freestyle riders like Mike Dominguez, Eddie Fiola, Stu Thompson and Harry Larry.

Growing up in the '80s we were also into cool bands, like Iron Maiden, AC/DC, Van Halen, Ratt and Mötley Crüe. Like the BMX guys, a couple of these bands were pinned to the walls in posters pulled from rock magazines like *Circus, Kerrang* or *Metal Edge*.

As I began fine-tuning my own bike, Scott reached over and pushed play on the tape deck of his "boom box"—a large, silver and black radio/tape player about the size of a small suitcase. Instantly the room was filled with the heavy opening riff and pounding drums of "Into the Fire." A moment later Don Dokken's vocals came in—I'll never forget it. "You weave your spell, your eyes they beckon me." I had no idea who the band was, but I was instantly hooked. As the tape played on I listened intently. I distinctively remember the songs, "When Heaven Comes Down," and

"Bullets to Spare." And that was all it took, after hearing *Tooth and Nail* I was a life-long Dokken fan.

A few days later I remember buying the album at the local Warehouse Records store and rockin' out to it in my bedroom.

Now for those who remember, and had the privilege of growing up in the '70s and '80s, buying a record was a special event. You would wait anxiously until its impending arrival—having heard about it on MTV or read about it in your favorite magazine. As kids we would ride our bikes over to a local record store like Licorice Pizza—a store that was entirely dedicated to selling records, tapes and videos—and spend time searching through rows and rows of records hoping to find a gem or a hard to get import.

Once you had your new record bagged up you would race home, anxious to get it on the turntable—but first you had to open it. Wanting to keep your record and its cover as mint as possible you would use a razor or knife to cut the plastic along the opening and gingerly pull out the record and its sleeve. A moment later, after the needle was dropped, you would sit back and enjoy the music while reading the liner notes and lyrics and checking out all the cool pics… Ahh, such great memories!

Fast forward three decades and I write my first book, a biography about former heavyweight champion Jersey Joe Walcott. I follow it up with another book about a former heavyweight champion Jack Sharkey. Having completed two boxing related books, I began thinking of a new subject to write about. It was then that I decided to turn my attention to another passion of mine—rock 'n' roll!

Ever since Ronnie James Dio's passing, writing a book about the legendary singer had been on my mind. So in November of 2016 I began the daunting task of writing the first full-length biography of Dio, which I completed in April of 2018. Writing the book was one of the best experiences of my life. What made it so much fun was all the great interviews; from Vivian Campbell to Tracy G. to Rowan Robertson and the late night marathon chats with Claude Schnell, they were all enjoyable and everybody was super nice.

Having had such a great time writing the Ronnie book, I decided to do another; all I had to do was find the right band. It took some time and a few months of consideration, but I eventually decided to do a book on Dokken. Since Jeff Pilson had written the foreword for the Ronnie book, I gave him my pitch. He liked the idea and was willing to help and do some interviews. From there I decided to get in touch with Don. To do this I reached out to Wendell Neeley, the host of *The Classic Metal Show* and good friend of Don Dokken. I told him what I wanted to do and was soon in e-mail contact with Don, who readily agreed to do some interviews.

Over the course of the next eight months I interviewed Don and Jeff a number of times. Both guys were gracious and more than willing to talk about their time in Dokken, and for that I am very thankful. In addition, I also interviewed former and current bandmates, friends and people who worked with Dokken and once again everyone was super friendly.

Unfortunately, Mick and George decided not to participate, which was a major bummer. However, I respected their decisions and even though I'm sure to get some backlash from fans who say, 'No George, no Mick, no Dokken book,' I decided to move forward without their input.

So, finally, after a year of writing and research the book is done. Much like the Dio book, this one was another fun writing adventure and I sincerely hope everyone who reads it gets as much pleasure out of Dokken's story as I had writing it.

James Curl
March 2020

Foreword

The Classic Metal Show gets called a lot of things... some nice, and others not so nice. One of the labels that the show gets is that we are "Dokken Groupies." While I certainly wouldn't consider myself a groupie, I'm definitely a fan of the band featuring Don Dokken, George Lynch, Jeff Pilson and "Wild" Mick Brown. I'd say that we are more "hardcore Dokken fans" than "Dokken groupies," but in the end, that's all just semantics. Unlike most people though, I was able to fulfill almost every rock 'n' roll dream I ever had because of my appreciation for the music this band created.

My love for Dokken music was why I started *The Classic Metal Show*; a show that has grown to be one of the most listened to, respected, feared and followed radio programs in the world of hard rock and metal today. Further, it led to a close personal friendship with vocalist Don Dokken. I'm not talking about the kind of relationship most people have where they get a complimentary handshake and a nod from their favorite band member; someone who's pretending they remember you from the other million people they meet each year on tour. No, my friendship has led to being asked to go out on tour with the band several times. I've sequenced multiple releases for them because Don trusts me to know what Dokken fans will like as much as he trusts his own ear to create those great songs. This all happened to a regular guy with a small dream and a love for the music created by a band that inspired him.

It was the fall of 1982 when I entered my first year of college. Since my parents were paying for my schooling, one of my responsibilities was to find a part-time job to help offset some of my living expenses. I applied for a job at a Camelot Music Store at the local mall since I had a passion for music. Simply working at a record store seemed like an exciting prospect to me. The opportunity to have access to the music of so many bands and artists both familiar and unfamiliar was a dream come true.

This was during the early stages of the newly launched MTV, which was rapidly having an impact on the musical landscape by changing the way people were discovering and consuming new music. The introduction of the music video as a mainstream outlet caused people to listen to their favorite music through their eyes as well as their ears. As a young music connoisseur, I too fell under the spell of the MTV music video.

Hard rock and heavy metal had a huge breakout year in 1983 as Def Leppard's *Pyromania,* Quiet Riot's *Metal Health*, Dio's *Holy Diver*, and Mötley Crüe's *Shout at the Devil* were racing up the music charts driven primarily by their exposure on MTV. One band in particular that caught my ear and eyes was Dokken. I remember unpacking *Breaking the Chains* while restocking the record bins and thinking how that black cover with the cool spiraling Dokken logo made a statement. The music video for "*Breaking the Chains*" was also getting some heavy rotation on MTV.

What could be cooler than the opening guitar riff of George Lynch's Tiger stripe guitar, Jeff Pilson's heavy bass line and "Wild" Mick Brown's thundering drums? How about the immediately identifiable lead vocals of singer Don Dokken? I was instantly hooked! The unique chemistry of these four musicians laid the groundwork for what would become the soundtrack of my life.

I continued to discover and follow many of the bands that were rising up in the music scene. Hard melodic rock was where it was at for me. The unfortunate demise of rock stalwarts Led Zeppelin in 1980 left a void that needed to be filled, and that hole was being filled quickly! Veteran bands such as Judas Priest, Scorpions, Y&T, Black Sabbath, Twisted Sister and AC/DC were enjoying newfound popularity during this time despite having careers that already spanned a decade.

Up and coming bands like Ratt, Queensrÿche, Bon Jovi, and Night Ranger were becoming radio and MTV staples. It was a great time in music history for any hard rock fan. In spite of the barrage of new music being released and promoted, Dokken continued to be my go to listen.

The release of *Tooth and Nail* in 1984 cemented my love and appreciation for Dokken. The craftsmanship and performance of the songs were nothing short of stellar. Although several of the songs on this release received the MTV video treatment, the song that stood out for me, even to this day is "When Heaven Comes Down." That heavy chugging guitar riff that opens the song followed by a monstrous drum fill still gives me a chill whenever I hear it. This song not only demonstrates the tight cohesiveness of a band firing on all cylinders, it gives you a glimpse of the driving force that Dokken would soon become in their follow up releases. The diverse song compositions of classic metal to melodic rock of *Tooth and Nail* makes for a fun listen.

Just when I didn't think Dokken could get any better, along came 1985's *Under Lock and Key*! Don Dokken's vocals backed with the harmonies of Jeff Pilson and "Wild" Mick coupled with the mastery of George Lynch's guitar forever solidified Dokken's trademark sound.

MTV had become a well-oiled machine by this time, and any band with credibility was being played and promoted on the channel. Dokken was no exception. The music videos for "In My Dreams" and "It's Not Love" quickly became favorites of mine. Even though MTV had been around for four years at this point, a video to promote a record or a song was still a fairly new concept.

The thrill of being able to see your favorite band performing a new song on TV right in your own living room was addictive. I remember going to Warehouse Music to pick up the cassette of *Under Lock and Key*. I played it endlessly. The two cassettes that dominated the player in my car that year were *Led Zeppelin's IV* and *Under Lock and Key*. I played *Under Lock and Key* so much I literally wore out two copies.

By the time 1987 rolled around, Dokken had become a heavy metal juggernaut. With the release of *Back for the Attack*, it was clear Dokken was on the path to become an arena headlining act, and deservedly so. *Back for the Attack* was an unusually long record, clocking in at just over an hour.

1987 was shaping up to be another huge year for hard rock and metal fans. Not only did we get *Back for the Attack,* but releases from Guns N' Roses, Whitesnake, Great White, Mötley Crüe, Dio, Def Leppard and Aerosmith were all dominating the music charts. This was an especially huge year for Dokken, as the song "Dream Warriors" was selected as the title track for the third installment of the *Nightmare on Elm Street* movie series.

There was no better promotion for a band than having a hit song on a popular movie soundtrack while receiving massive exposure with a music video to promote it. After 33 years, Dokken is still synonymous with the iconic villain Freddy Krueger. I remember going to see *Nightmare on Elm Street part 3* and waiting until the credits finished rolling, just to watch the music video for "Dream Warriors" at the end while the theater cleared out!

In 1988, Dokken were at their peak. They were selected as one of the participants of the Monsters of Rock Stadium Tour, which featured rock titans Van Halen and Scorpions, along with up and coming bands Metallica and Kingdom Come. Little did I know as a fan that cracks were forming within the Dokken camp that would ultimately lead to their demise. At the end of the Monsters of Rock tour, my favorite band was no more. Since this was pre-internet, it was difficult to get information on what was happening with your favorite bands. You had to rely on music publications like *RIP, Circus, Creem* or *Metal Edge.* If you were living in a city like Los Angeles as I was at the time, you might have the good fortune of catching your favorite band or artist during an interview on one of the radio stations that supported rock and metal.

The '80s were a great time for rock radio in Los Angeles as KLOS, KMET, KCAL and KNAC were all exemplary rock stations. There were also great syndicated radio shows like Metal Shop hosted by Charlie Kendall and Rockline hosted by Bob Coburn. These radio shows kept rock fans in the loop as far as news about your favorite bands as well as hard rock and metal in general. These shows were highly influential in my life and planted the seeds for things to come.

In October of 1990, after almost a two-year hiatus Don Dokken reemerged with a new offering under his own name. *Up from the Ashes* was a welcome release for those who were missing the music of Dokken. I remember going to the Sam Goody music store in the mall and purchasing the CD. CDs were a new format for me as I'd always purchased LPs or cassette tapes. This was the first CD I ever purchased, and I still have it in my collection. I really enjoyed *Up from the Ashes* as it seemed to pick right back up where *Back for the Attack* left off.

The prospect of seeing Don Dokken perform live again was exciting, but unfortunately the opportunity to catch the *Up from the Ashes* tour never came to pass. I was driving on the I-10 freeway in L.A. one fall afternoon listening to KLOS, and Don was in the studio promoting the release of *Up from the Ashes*. The radio station was running a contest as part of the promotion, which included a chance to "Have lunch with Don Dokken." I just knew I had to enter that contest! This was in the days where you had to send in a postcard to be entered in the drawing. As soon as I got home I filled out and mailed my postcard. Although I wasn't the winning contestant, as fate would have it, my day would eventually come.

1991 was a pivotal year for me. Due to a change in employment and personal circumstances, I left California and went out on the road as a cross country truck driver. This gave me a lot of time to reflect and think about where I wanted to be in life and what would truly make me happy. Oftentimes the radio or my CD collection were my only friends. Since I travelled from coast to coast, I was able to listen to quite a cross section of radio programming and a wide variety of disc jockeys. This experience made one thing very clear! There was a lot of bad radio out there… at least for a person like me. This was also during a shift in the music scene when "grunge" was the popular genre, while hard melodic rock and metal were deemed passé'. I made up my mind that once I got my priorities back in line, I was going to get off the road, go to broadcasting school and start my own radio show that would feature the hard rock and metal that I thrived on.

Fast forward to 1995. After four years of driving a truck, I had saved enough money to pay for the full year of tuition to attend The Ohio Center For Broadcasting. I had already made up my mind that I was going to get off the road at the end of June and start broadcasting school in July.

In the late winter or early spring of 1995, I was parked at a shopping mall waiting to be dispatched on a new trucking load when I decided to kill some time by going into the mall and walking around. I stopped into a record store, and as I was looking through the CDs, I noticed they had an import section, which often has rare or hard to find releases. As I was perusing the CDs, I came across a Japanese import of Dokken: *One Live Night.* I picked that CD up and looked at it thinking, 'When did they record this? Are Dokken back together?' I couldn't believe it! Being on the road all the time, if there was some kind of announcement, I was not aware of it. I purchased the CD and took it out to my truck and put it in the CD player immediately! What I heard was absolutely amazing! I couldn't believe I missed this!

It was a Friday night in late April and I was coming out of Chicago on my way home for the weekend when I was passing through Toledo, Ohio. I was listening to the local Toledo rock station WIOT when I heard the DJ announce 'Coming to Roxann's Saturday May 6, Dokken!' I couldn't believe it. Dokken was back together and touring! There is no way I was going to miss this!

When I got home, I called the club asking how I could get tickets for the show. The guy on the phone said that they were selling them at the club and various music stores around Toledo. I explained that I was coming in from out of town and I didn't have any way of purchasing them locally beforehand. The guy on the phone told me he was the club owner, and said he would set a couple tickets aside with my name on them, and I could pay for them at the door. Score!

On Saturday May 6, I made the two-hour trip from Akron, Ohio where I was living to Toledo to catch the show. I was a little early because I wanted to scope out the club to make sure I knew where it was before going to get dinner before the show. I pulled into the parking lot, and just as I did I saw Mick Brown getting out of a pickup truck. I got out of the car to say hello, and Mick greeted me like we were long lost friends even though I had never met him before. I had the CD cover of *Tooth and Nail* with me which he gladly signed, and said, 'I'll see you at the show, thanks for making the trip!'

When the club opened, I went up to the box office window and gave the guy my name. It was the club owner I had spoken to on the phone and he immediately asked, 'How was the trip over? Glad you were able to make it. Enjoy the show!' What a show it was! Seeing Dokken back together performing live was like reclaiming a lost part of my life. I realize that sounds dramatic, but Dokken music carried me through both good and bad times and as I said at the beginning, it is the soundtrack of my life. The show was a combination of in your face rockers as well as an acoustic set similar to what I heard on *One Live Night*. What a great night to be Rokkin' With Dokken again!

As I was leaving the club, I just happened to run into the club owner. He recognized me and started asking me how I enjoyed the show? He was walking around to the back of the club where Dokken's tour bus was parked, so I just walked along with him past the security guards who were guarding the entrance. He thanked me again for coming out but said he had to go take care of a few things. I walked over to the tour bus where there were four or five people hanging out talking with Jeff Pilson. He was signing autographs and taking pictures, so I gave him my *Tooth and Nail* CD cover to sign. He said he was going to go back in the bus, but to hang out because Don would be out in a few minutes.

I waited around and Don eventually came out of the bus to meet the few people who were hanging out to say hello. The remaining fans were asking for autographs but only had scraps of paper or dollar bills to sign using a ballpoint pen. Don was having trouble signing autographs with a pen and asked, 'Doesn't anyone have a Sharpie?' I had brought two Sharpies with me, so I said, 'Don, if I can talk with you for a couple minutes, you can have my Sharpies.' Don put his arm around my shoulder and we walked away from the other fans and he said, "What's up?" I told him who I was and explained to him that as a fan of Dokken, hard rock and metal, Dokken was the inspiration for me to go to broadcasting school. I then explained my goal of having my own show that would feature bands like Dokken, since no one was playing them at that moment. Don seemed intrigued, and asked me to keep in touch and let him know how things were going.

True to my word, I followed through with completing broadcasting school and launching *The Classic Metal Show* on January 6, 1996. The show has lasted a quarter century. It's featured several co-hosts, thousands of interviews, and has been the gateway for me to not only meet just about every rock star I ever wanted to meet, but also becoming friendly with so many of them. At its core though, the show was built from my love of Dokken's music, and it remains that way today.

Speaking of those friendships, it's been almost 25 years since I first met Don and formed a lifelong friendship with him. He has been my biggest inspiration for starting and continuing *The Classic Metal Show* after all these years. I have also had the pleasure of knowing and forming longtime friendships with both Jeff Pilson and "Wild" Mick Brown. My life has truly been blessed knowing these guys through their music as well as on a personal level.

In the end, I am the same as everyone reading this book. I was just a fan of a band whose music truly moved me. Unlike most though, I turned it into the most fulfilling, fun part of my life for the last 25 years. To paraphrase a Dokken song, I'll be a fan and supporter "Until The Living End."

Wendell Neeley
Host, *The Classic Metul Show*
March 26, 2020

Chapter 1
The Sunset Strip

The 1980s were a glorious time for hard rock and heavy metal, particularly in Los Angeles, California. The famous Sunset Strip in L.A. was the place to be if you were an aspiring "Rock Star," or just a fan. In America, it was the center of the universe for a booming musical movement, and anyone who was anyone was there. But, long before the '80s came the Strip had already enjoyed a rich and colorful history that was both illustrious and infamous.

The mile and a half stretch of road, officially known as "Sunset Boulevard," first came to prominence in the 1920s and runs right through the heart of West Hollywood. With the rise of motion pictures and movie stars, night clubs and casinos began opening up along the Strip. They offered a playground for celebrities and made it the ultimate entertainment spot in L.A.

During this time the Strip was outside the city's borders and was therefore beyond the reach of the LAPD's jurisdiction. This absence of rules beyond the city limits brought in the gangster element and their ilk. With Prohibition being the law of the land during the '20s and early '30s the lack of law enforcement led to the emergence of hidden speakeasies where illegal booze flowed freely. This created an environment that transformed the "Strip" into a free-for-all zone where people left their inhibitions at the front door.

Throughout the '40s and '50s the Strip's popularity increased exponentially as it continued to expand with restaurants, boutiques and hotels. Ciro's, the Mocambo and the Trocadero were part of a galaxy of well-known and glamorous nightclubs that were frequented by socialites and Hollywood's elite. Frank Sinatra, Eva Gardner, Humphrey Bogart, Clark Gable and Marilyn Monroe were just a few who hung out on the Strip. Some of the upper class nightclubs like The Melody Room were reputed to be gambling havens for mobsters and were rumored to be owned "behind the scenes" by notorious gangsters like Mickey Cohen and Bugsy Siegel.

By the 1960s the Strip had lost much of its appeal with film stars. Instead, its many restaurants and clubs became a mecca for tourists and young people who were part of the hippie and rock 'n' roll counter-culture. More importantly, several clubs of note opened during this period. The Whisky a Go Go, The Roxy, Pandora's Box, Gazzaris and the Rainbow Bar and Grill were but a few that would go on to become historically iconic.

The Rainbow in particular would become famous for a variety of reasons. Before it was the Rainbow it was the Villa Nova where baseball great Joe DiMaggio and Marilyn Monroe met on a blind date in 1952. In 1972 the Villa Nova closed and reopened as the Rainbow on April 16 with a party for Elton John—it became an instant hit.

In the mid-'70s its upstairs section known as "Over the Rainbow" was an exclusive hangout for big-name rock stars. It would eventually be dubbed "The Lair of the Hollywood Vampires," by a group of drinking buddies made up of, Alice Cooper (president), the Who's Keith Moon, songwriter Harry Nilsson, the Monkees' Mickey Dolenz, John Lennon,

Ringo Starr, Neil Diamond and honorary members Jimi Hendrix and Jim Morrison.

By all accounts these rockers spent so much time in the Rainbow that they rarely saw daylight; hence the nickname "Hollywood Vampires."

It was at the Rainbow that Ronnie James Dio and Ritchie Blackmore dreamt up their band Rainbow—named after and in honor of their favorite hangout. It was also at the Rainbow that John Belushi ate his last meal of Lentil soup, before overdosing on cocaine and heroin.

As a result of the Strip's booming popularity during the 1960s, traffic congestion, late night disturbances and drug abuse had local residents and business owners irritated. Demanding a solution, the city administrators hoped to curb the crowds of young club patrons by instituting a strict 10:00 p.m. curfew. They also rescinded the "youth permits" of twelve of the Strip's clubs, thereby making them off-limits to anybody under 21. Furthermore, Pandora's Box, one of the most popular clubs on the Strip, would be closed and demolished.

These actions however were perceived by the youth as a violation of their civil rights, which caused growing tension and protests.

On November 12, 1966 over 1,000 people rallied to protest the closing of Pandora's Box including Sonny and Cher, who got their start on the Strip. Actor Jack Nicholson was there as a curious observer as was Peter Fonda who was filming the event.

The protest began peacefully but turned violent after a fender bender involving a group of off duty Marines. After breaking up the fight, police closed off part of the Strip and ordered everyone to leave. Some of the protesters began to run amok. They threw bottles and rocks through storefront windows, and rocked a city bus until the frightened passengers and driver got off. As a result numerous people were arrested. The protesting continued for the next few weeks, but eventually subsided and a number of clubs closed their doors. The riots inspired Steven Stills of Buffalo Springfield to pen the now famous song, "For What It's Worth."

The riots did little to diminish the Strip's popularity. In fact, it quickly regained its composure. With so many clubs offering a spot to play music the Strip remained a hot-spot for emerging talent. Local bands like Canned Heat and the Turtles got their start during this time, and the Doors got their first real gig at the London Fog. Led Zeppelin, Frank Zappa, The Byrds, the Who and Jimi Hendrix all spent time playing the clubs during the late '60s and into the early 1970s.

By the mid-'70s rock 'n' roll began to lose some of its hold on the Strip. With the rise of disco and the popularity of British "glam rock" clubs like Rodney Bingenheimer's English Disco became increasingly popular. They catered to the "glitter rock" crowd and groups like Iggy Pop and the Stooges, Sweet, and the New York Dolls were frequent players.

By the late '70s "glitter rock" had run its course and new wave and punk, became the music of choice. Bands like Devo, the Ramones, Blondie, the Talking Heads and the Knack had captured everyone's attention and were playing the prime times at the clubs.

As the 1970s came to a close the Strip braced itself for a new and exciting decade—the 1980s. The new era would prove to be unlike any before it. The '80s would push the limits of the Strip to a new height of popularity and debauchery and in doing so would earn its nickname, "The Decade of Decadence." And rock 'n' roll, particularly hard rock and heavy metal, would come roaring back to grab hold of the Strip with a leather studded hand.

The burgeoning decade would also give rise to an unparalleled number of hard rock and heavy metal bands as well as numerous sub genres. These bands unabashedly ruled the era with spandex, leather and big hair. But make no mistake, for all the depravity and excesses of "sex, drugs and rock 'n' roll," most of the bands that emerged were talented. Moreover, the virtuosity of guitar playing in particular was brought to a level that had never been witnessed before and may never be seen again.

At the same time that rock was making its comeback on the Sunset Strip, over in Europe the New Wave of British heavy metal was revving up and gaining momentum. Groups like Iron Maiden, Def Leppard, Motörhead, Saxon, and Venom were having a major influence on the sound and style of emerging bands in America. Most of the NWOBHM bands would eventually play the Strip and a few of them like Iron Maiden and Def Leppard would achieve mega-stardom. Though most of the bands would never become "household names" they bequeathed an influence that lasted for years and helped usher in a truly magical decade.

During the early '80s dozens of bands were jockeying for position and climbing the rungs of a ladder that led straight up to fame and superstardom. Van Halen, Ratt, Mötley Crüe, Guns N' Roses and Quiet Riot, along with many more, paid their dues playing the Strip.

Places like, The Starwood, The Whisky a Go Go and the Troubadour were filled to capacity nightly. Raucous crowds of long-haired head bangers and groupies in mini-skirts and fishnet stockings swarmed in by the thousands. Lines of eager fans, wanting to see their favorite bands, snaked around the neon nightclubs and the Strip was so crowded that it rivaled rush hour in New York City. At times, the clubs were so jam-packed that the throngs of people spilled out onto the busy sidewalks where the party continued. While inside the clubs, screeching guitars mixed with booming drums, melodic vocals, and the screams of fans in a distorted frenzy of drink, smoke and music.

Greg Leon, vocalist and guitarist for Suite 19 and the Greg Leon Invasion was a regular at the Whisky a Go Go and remembers the Strip well. "It was unbelievable, it was just nut to butt people all up and down the Strip from like Clark Street from where the Whisky is at all the way to Turner's liquor store. And there would be thousands of kids almost seven out of seven nights. There would be bands playing and bands on the street handing out their flyers. You know, people hanging out in the parking lot at the Rainbow. It was just fun. There were girls everywhere, there were guys everywhere. Everyone was dressed to the nines. And everybody thought they were gonna be the next big star."[1]

Jack Russell, former vocalist and founding member of Great White remembers the Strip fondly saying, "There were thousands of people on the Strip, literally thousands up and down Santa Monica Boulevard, up and down Sunset Boulevard. It was electric, you could do no wrong, we owned it. What I would do—it would be a Friday afternoon and I

---

1 Greg Leon interview with James Curl.

would have a friend of mine drop me off up at the Rainbow parking lot or the Whisky parking lot. And he would be like, 'Well how you gonna get home?' and I would say, 'Don't worry about it, I'll figure out a way.'

"And I would end up going to a party and going to another party and end up with some chicks and going to another party, you know. And somehow I would end up getting back to Orange County with a couple chicks. It was a gas and we did whatever we wanted to and there was nobody to say shit about it. You know there was no decade like it, there never will be. Rock 'n' roll will never be as big."[2]

With the metal scene really starting to explode by 1983, a number of the Strip bands like Quiet Riot, Mötley Crüe, W.A.S.P and Ratt were already having great success. One band in particular that had been in the mix for several years but hadn't quite "broken out" was Dokken. They were, however, about to hit big.

Though frequently tossed in with the typical "hair metal" bands of the '80s, Dokken was really much more than that. In fact, they had more substance and far more talent than most. Dokken's unique mixture of hi-energy rock, coupled with melodic guitar melodies and soaring vocals set them apart from the majority. During the mid-80s, Dokken would become one of the biggest bands to emerge from L.A. and help fuel the meteoric rise of the L.A metal scene.

During the "Decade of Decadence" they would achieve incredible success and realize terrible lows. But through it all Don, Jeff, Mick and George would help create some of the most memorable music of a generation.

---

2 Jack Russell interview with James Curl.

Chapter 2
Beginnings

Dokken was founded by vocalist Donald Maynard "Don" Dokken. The future frontman was born June 29, 1953 in Los Angeles, California. At the time of his birth his parents were only teenagers. "Had a mother and father," said Don, "but they were 16 when I was born. My dad got shipped off to Korea and my mom got shipped off to the nut house, she had a nervous breakdown at a young age."[3] As a result Don was placed into an orphanage.

"I went to an orphanage when I was five years old with my brother," said Don. "As far as my music, it was all by accident. I got out of the orphanage and went to foster homes and about the third or fourth foster home the father of the foster home was a drummer and he let me go in the garage and bang on his drums, so I learned how to play drums first."[4]

Being in foster care wasn't easy, and didn't afford a lot of privacy. Don typically found himself living with several other foster kids, and sharing a crowded room stacked to the ceiling with bunk beds. As a way to cope, and get a little time to himself, Don would use music to escape. As a young boy he listened to bands like the Kinks, the Beau Brummels and the Strawberry Alarm Clocks on his record player.

"Then I went back with my mom but I couldn't have a drum set. So she took me to a pawn shop and said pick any instrument that you want, and I picked the guitar. I was about twelve. So I just did the thing a lot of people did. I just went

---

3 YouTube interview, Don Dokken, part (1 of 5).
4 Don Dokken interview with James Curl.

in the garage with my little amplifier, my silvertone, made by Sears. My silvertone guitar and I had a little record player that played 45s and I played the Kinks and the Moody Blues and I just learned how to play guitar by playing to the songs, and that's how I got started."[5]

"The first album I ever bought was the first Cream album, "Fresh Cream" (1966) and I listened to it over and over and over and I'd slow it down and try to copy Eric Clapton's guitar parts and that's when I started really playing guitar seriously."[6]

In 8th grade as part of a class project, Don played his first concert, handling both vocals and guitar, while a classmate pounded the skins. Together the two young boys did their best cover of the song "Louie, Louie," by the Kingsmen.

For Don, music came naturally, in fact the talent for it ran deep in his family.

"My father was a professional musician, played in a jazz band, trombonist and singer. He played into his 70s the Jerry Dokken orchestra and he played jazz his whole life. My mother was a piano player, her mother was a guitar player and my mother's father was a guitar player. So there was music on both sides of the family."[7]

Back with his mother, Don would spent the majority of his childhood around the poor sections of Venice, California. He attended Venice high school and eventually moved to Manhattan Beach.

As Don got a little older his taste in music matured and his interests broadened. As a teenager he got into bands like

---

5 Ibid.
6 *Blabbermouth,* Don Dokken slam "stupid Kardashians," denies sleeping with Bobby Blotzer's ex-wife, November 9th, 2015.
7 Don Dokken interview with James Curl.

Led Zeppelin, Deep Purple, the Beatles and Jimi Hendrix. He also developed a love of cars, particularly muscle cars and Corvettes—and it was during this time that he learned how to bust his knuckles wrenching on them. "I built my first car at 13. A '56 Chevy I bought for like $25 dollars. I had the manual and figured it out. I like cars and I've built a lot of cars in my life, but it's just fun and a hobby."

As a youth, one of Don's early jobs was working as a cook. "My uncle was kind of a famous chef, my uncle Bud," said Don. "He ran the Ambassador hotel which was a famous hotel in Downton L.A. He cooked for all the presidents, Kennedy and all those people. And he ran a couple restaurants down on Hermosa Beach where I was living.

"I started out as a waiter and washing dishes, then I started making salads. Then my uncle put me on the grill and started teaching me how to flip an egg without breaking the yolk and how to cook an omelet and a hamburger. And how to tell if a steak is medium, or medium rare just by touching the meat. I became a cook for about five years and luckily there were like four rock clubs four blocks away. And I would go down and I would cook till about eight or nine at night, then I'd grab my guitar and go down to the clubs and jam with Mick Mars. Mick was playing the circuit at the same time, before Mötley Crüe he was in a band called Vendetta and he would do five sets a night and Mick would call me and say, 'Hey, could you come down and play the last set? Cause I'm toast.'

"So, I would go down and play the Deep Purple set at midnight and sit in with Vendetta and Mick Mars. And after that I went and started working for a body shop, a place called One Day Body Shop and I learned how to work on cars and do body work."[8]

Eventually, Don found his way to Manhattan Beach. "I moved down to Manhattan Beach and had a bunch of roommates and it turned out that all my roommates were musicians. My best friend I went to high school with was Armando Acosta, who was the drummer in Saint Vitas and we jammed together in garages. The same old shit everyone did; you know, we would jam on the weekends in the garage."[9] While living in Manhattan Beach, Don worked as a cook. "I worked for several years as a cook at a place in Manhattan Beach called the Kettle, graveyard shift."[10]

"I have fond memories of me walking two miles before I had a driver's license with my amp and my guitar, and I would go steal a shopping cart and use the shopping cart to wheel my equipment to rehearsal two miles away. And we would play and practice and Armando was my roommate and other musicians were living there, and we all just jammed in the living room. That's where I met Bobby Blotzer. We ordered pizzas one night and Bobby was working for Dominos or something and he delivered a pizza to us and he saw the drum set and he sat down and we jammed for a while. And that's how he became the first drummer for Airborn."[11]

By the time 1976 rolled around Don, who was all of 22, was a regular on the Sunset Strip playing in his first band called Airborn. As leader of the band, Don took care of vocals and guitar while Bobby Blotzer pounded the drums and Jeff Tappan played bass.

---

8 Ibid.
9 Ibid.
10 Ibid
11 Ibid.

This pre-Dokken band played all the hot-spots like the Starwood, the Troubadour and the Whisky a Go-Go. Remembering the time, Don said, "We warmed up for Journey, Y&T, a lot of famous bands—Santana."[12]

Tall and lean with brown, shoulder length hair, vibrant blue eyes and handsome features, Don fit the required image of a great front man. But more importantly he had a unique voice, one that set him apart from the typical singers that haunted the smoky night clubs. In addition to his family's musical pedigree, he also had an innate talent for writing lyrics and was well versed when it came to composing songs.

At this particular time there were only a handful of rock bands playing the Strip and it hadn't yet exploded into the phenomenon that it would become in the '80s. "There was Van Halen, Quiet Riot, and Me," said Don. "The original members of Ratt were in Dokken, Warren DeMartini played in Dokken, Frankie Benali from Quiet Riot played in Dokken, Juan Croucier and Bobby Blotzer from Ratt played in Dokken. We were all just fighting it out for 50 bucks."[13]

Over time, Jeff eventually left Airborn and Juan Croucier stepped in as his replacement. Not making enough money playing gigs, Don also worked at an auto body shop and was at this point more or less only playing for fun on the weekends. "Looking back," said Don, "I thought if we could sell out the Whisky a Go-Go, we would have accomplished our goal."[14]

---

12 Ibid.
13 YouTube interview with Don Dokken, August 15, 2008 (2 of 5).
14 An Interview with Don Dokken of Dokken, January 5, 2017, by Julian Douglas.

The lineup of Don, Bobby and Juan lasted until late 1977, when Bobby and Juan decided to jump ship and form their own band called Firefoxx.

It was around this time that another band using the name Airborn, albeit with an "e" at the end, was signed to a record deal. Because of this circumstance, Don was forced to relinquish the name and decided to simply go with Dokken. "We didn't really have a name for the band," said Don, "so I just started calling it Dokken."[15]

To replace Bobby and Juan, Don recruited drummer Greg Pecka and bassist Steven R. Barry. Remembering how he joined Dokken, Steven said, "How I met Don was through Drake Levin, (former guitarist for Paul Revere & the Raiders) the original producer for Dokken. He had a music store in Manhattan Beach called Drake's music. I moved out to Southern California in July of '77 and I want to say this was probably near the end of '77 when I finally got all my basses sent out and finally got a place to live.

"And I went to buy some strings and Drake said, 'I'm producing a new band that needs a bass player.' I ended up meeting Don that night at his house and played him some things I'd done and showed him some photos of the bands I'd been in, and we went out and had a couple of drinks and I was in from then on. This was the first version of Dokken to my knowledge, he had just changed it from Airborn."[16]

Together the trio recorded and released the very first Dokken record, a 7″ single produced by Drake Levin in 1979 with the song, "Hard Rock Woman" on side A and "Broken Heart" on the B side.

---

15 Don Dokken interview with James Curl.
16 Steven R. Barry interview with James Curl.

"We did the 45″ at Hermosa Beach at Media Arts which was above a bar we played at called Shenanigans," said Steven.

By the latter part of the '70s the popularity of rock 'n' roll was waning in America and particularly on the Strip. A new scene was evolving and bands like, Devo, Elvis Costello, the Plimsouls and Blondie were gaining immense popularity. "You couldn't get a job in L.A. playing heavy metal," said Don. "They called it 'dinosaur rock.' See, this is when the Knack was really peaking. Heavy metal was on Monday nights, Monday nights at the Troubadour."[17]

As rock's popularity declined and new wave and punk took over, Don had the opportunity in late 1979 to go to Germany, where rock was still the music of choice.

"Some people were here in L.A from Germany," said Don, "Michael and Betina Boyens, and they were building a rock club in Hamburg, and they were looking at different clubs trying to figure out how they were going to design theirs. They saw me play and said you should come to Germany, rock is really popular there.[18]

"So, Michael booked me a tour; so, we hocked everything and went to Germany and did that little tour and that was the beginning." However, two weeks before leaving for Germany, Steven gave Don the bad news that he would be unable to do the tour. Remembering the moment Don replied, "I said wait a minute, we booked the tickets, we're going, the shows are booked." Scrambling to find a replacement, Don gave Juan a call. "And so I called Juan, who lived three blocks from me. Juan wasn't doing anything

---

17 Dokken, interview by Joy Williams, *Artist Magazine.*
18 Don Dokken interview with James Curl.

and so he joined the band. We rehearsed for a week and off we went to Germany."[19]

Explaining why he couldn't go to Germany and when he left Dokken, Steven said, "I left right before the German tour of later '79 and I had a child that was due December 28, my very first child. Don wanted me to go over early to Germany to do promos and stuff, but that was when my kid was going to be born, so I told him 'if you can take Greg over, and I can stay home I'll meet you there,' but he wasn't having it another way. So we kinda got into it and he and I never had a squabble in the band ever, you know what I mean? I know he's kinda known for having squabbles with bandmates but he and I had a good friendship until that day he decided I had to go. He offered me more money to go, but I said, 'dude, it's not money. I can be there before the tour starts, but I just want to be here when my son's born and I'll catch up.' "[20]

As a three-piece power trio, Don, Juan and Greg spent a couple of weeks gigging and enjoying the German hospitality. "We played The Star club, The Chicago club, The Top Ten club—all the famous clubs where the Beatles played," said Don. "That was where I met Lemmy Kilmister from Motörhead for the first time. I said, 'I'm from L.A., and man, you're Lemmy!' He said, 'You buying?' We drank all night."

It was while in Germany that Don became acquainted with Michael Wagener, a young up-and-coming producer who was working with the German band Accept. Michael had actually been the original guitarist for Accept but had been drafted into the German Army when he turned 18.

---

19 Ibid.
20 Steven R. Barry interview with James Curl.

Unfortunately for Michael, he was stationed over 350 miles away from his bandmates, which made attending practices impossible.

After completing 24 months, Michael returned home in 1972 and began working as an audio engineer in Hamburg. "I had a studio in Hamburg, Germany," recalls Michael on his first meeting with Don, "and we were hooked up to record at a club right next door, they were playing the club so we recorded him. And then afterwards Don and I got together and did some more recording in the studio. And that's how we met."[21]

Having become fast friends, Don and Michael continued to hang out and record. Often, after playing shows all night, Don and his bandmates along with Michael would head into the studio and cut demos until the early morning hours. Six of these demos, along with a couple of live bootleg recordings, were later stolen and illegally released as an EP called, Dokken: *Back in the Streets*. "Someone made a lot of money off that bootleg," said Don.[22]

Having finished their first club tour of Germany, Dokken headed back to the States, but not before inviting Michael to come to L.A for a visit. "I said, Michael, come to America, you're so talented, you should just come to America." Don explained to his new friend that L.A had a renowned music scene and suggested that there would probably be work for a guy with Michael's abilities.

Back home, Dokken continued playing the Sunset. About three weeks later Michael showed up for a short vacation

---

21 Michael Wagener interview with James Curl.
22 Don Dokken talks early days, acoustic shows and much more, by John Parks, December 7, 2012.

over the Christmas holidays and crashed on Don's couch. At this time Don was living with his girlfriend Eva in a small two-bedroom apartment. After spending some time in L.A., and seeing that the music scene had a lot of potential, Michael decided that he wanted to come back and stay permanently. A quick trip home to Germany ensued and by March of 1980 Michael had returned.

Together, Don and Michael worked the music scene, but the pay was hardly enough to live on. To help supplement their income and pay the bills the two also hustled cars. "We worked together buying and selling cars," said Don.

"So, Michael came to live with me and we had nothing. We had no money—I had nothing. So, I'm a mechanic and there was this paper that used to be around called the Penny Saver. And you couldn't sell anything above one hundred dollars—that was the limit. And I'd see a '73 Chevy van for a $100 bucks. We'd go check it out and I'd buy it. It was all dented up, the paint is all fucked up. I said, 'Don't worry, Michael, we can make this happen.' And we were so poor we couldn't afford masking tape. So, I would just buy like six cans of primer, primer the whole van grey. I would try and keep as much paint off the windows as possible and Michael would be out there with steel wool getting the paint off the windshield. Our fingers were raw from steel wooling.

"And the van smokes like a motherfuck and I say, 'I know a trick.' We would put 90w standard transmission oil in it and it wouldn't smoke. It's like glue; it seals all the valve guides and all the O-rings and it cuts the smoking down. We would then buy black fabric dye, spray the whole interior of the van for about $20 bucks, spray the seats, spray the dash and we would sell it for like $800 bucks or $400 bucks and I'm like, well we just made $400 bucks, there's our rent."[23]

"That's right," said Michael, "we were buying, painting and selling cars, you gotta pay the rent, right?"[24]

Eventually, Michael found a job as a maintenance engineer at Larrabee Sound Studio. The money however wasn't great, so Michael took a job that was offered to work with the band Accept. "Udo Dirkschneider came for a vacation to America and offered me to do the live sound for Accept in Europe. So, I went back to Germany knowing I would return to the USA sooner or later."[25]

It wasn't long after Michael left that Dokken headed back to Germany for another tour in late 1980. During the previous tour in '79, Dokken had been appointed a tour manager named Neiko. Neiko had worked with the Scorpions on their first American tour as a photographer and interpreter because he spoke English. He was also well acquainted with Dieter Dirks, the Scorpions' producer. While Dokken was in Germany during their first tour, Neiko had given a copy of the 7″ single "Hard Rock Woman" to Dieter. After hearing the record, Dieter had expressed some interest in it. "Neiko told me 'Dieter likes your little 45,' " said Don, 'and if you ever come back again he would like to see you play.'[26]

"So, I booked another tour in 1980 a year later and Juan didn't want to go, he was having relationship issues, and Greg Pecka was a Scientologist and he said, 'you know, I

23 Don Dokken interview with James Curl.
24 Michael Wagener interview with James Curl.
25 Michael Wagener biographical information.
26 Don Dokken interview with James Curl.

can't really go to Germany again, and if I go I'll get in trouble with the church.'[27]

"So, at the last minute I found Greg Leon on guitar, Gary Holland on drums and a guy named Gary Link, a bass player I found in a club. So, I put that band together, we rehearsed for like 10 days and off we went to Germany again, only because I wanted Dieter Dirks to see us play."[28]

Greg Leon remembers the time saying, "I think the first time Don saw me play was '77 or '78, we were playing at a club called the Rock Corporation in Van Nuys, California and we were opening up for him.

"I remember Don sitting out there watching me play that night. And when everything was getting loaded in the van my roadies accidentally loaded in his Marshall heads thinking they were mine. The next day I get a call from Don saying, 'Hey, this is Don Dokken, we played together last night. I think you got my Marshall heads.' I said, 'I don't think so, I'll go check the equipment van, call me back.' He called me back and I said, 'yeah, sure enough I do have them.' So he came up to the house and said, 'I love your style, I love your voice. I think it would be awesome if we did something together.' "[29] At the time though Greg was busy working with Kevin DuBrow of Quiet Riot, so he couldn't get anything going with Don. A few months later, however, Greg had quit the Quiet Riot lineup and when Don called he was ready.

"So I left that band," said Greg, "and I was in the process of thinking what my next step was, whether to go back and

---

27 Ibid.
28 Ibid.
29 Greg Leon interview with James Curl.

do my own thing or join somebody else's band, and Don got in touch with me again and said, 'Hey, I got a bunch of European dates.' He told me we were leaving in 21 days, so we started rehearsals and I brought my drummer at the time from the band Suite 19, Gary Holland and we joined the band, rehearsed like crazy and 21 days later we were on a plane to Europe.

"So anyways, we went over there and they had a place to put us up over this pub in Hamburg, Germany and we went out to do the shows from there. They put together an equipment truck for us and a couple of roadies and we did a bunch of shows over there and just knocked'em dead."[30]

Gary Link recalls the tour and the moment he first heard that John Lennon had been killed. "We flew over there and we ended up staying at Michael Boyen's sister's inn called the Melone. And we stayed upstairs of her little bar and that was where we were based. Michael was a keyboard player and promotor and ended up opening up for us at a couple of different places.

"The night we played the Top Ten club there was a lady there handing out towels as you come out of the bathroom and she was there when the Beatles played there. That night if you're looking at the stage Don was in the center, Greg was on the left, I was on the right and of course the drummer was in the back. So, I was on the right where Lennon actually was with the Beatles. The next morning, after we played there, we got up and went downstairs because the other band showed up and came over for breakfast and everyone kinda had their heads hanging and they went talking and they were really sad. And we're like, 'what's going on?' and they said

---

30 Ibid.

you didn't hear? Lennon got shot. So, I was on his spot on the stage and the next morning he got shot and killed. It was kinda weird."[31]

While in Germany, Don was lucky enough to have Dieter come down and see him play. "Dieter flew into Hamburg for one night," said Don, "had a five hour layover, came to our club and saw us play that night." After watching the performance, Dieter was impressed with Dokken. "Dieter came out to see us," said Greg "and he thought we were great. So we ended up at his studio in Cologne, Germany and did a five or six song demo."[32]

Following the German tour, Dokken returned to L.A and continued to gig up and down the Strip. "So we get back to the States," said Greg, "and we were playing the Starwood and some Whisky shows, and we did some showcases and we were getting some interest—people were talking about us. And every time we played a gig these record company people would come up to me and Don and say, 'Van Halen was the last guitar band we're gonna sign, so you guys should start thinking about listening to the new music that is coming out, like Devo and the Knack.' And they named all these new wave bands and they told us to cut our hair, and get rid of the leather and denim. And Don and I are looking at each other like, 'what the fuck are you talking about? We just came from Europe and people were going nuts for us."[33]

With no intention of taking the record label's advice, Dokken continued to play shows. But despite their best efforts, the guys were having no luck attaining the elusive

---

31 Gary Link interview with James Curl.
32 Greg Leon interview with James Curl.
33 Ibid.

title of "Rock Stars." Moreover, they were passed up several times by various record labels. As a result, the guys became discouraged and the band was on the verge of breaking up. Nevertheless, Don's fortunes were about to change.

In early 1981 while playing a show at the Whisky, Dieter Dierks just happened to walk in. After watching the band's performance, he and Don spent some time talking. "I'll never forget he said, 'I don't like your band.' And I went, 'well that's the end of that.' But he said, 'I like you. I like your voice, I like your guitar playing.' " Dieter then asked Don if he would like to come to Germany and sing backup vocals on a new Scorpion's album. The producer went on to explain that Klaus Mein, lead singer for the group, was being treated for nodes on his vocal cords. In fact, he was going to have surgery and would be unable to sing for some time. As compensation, Dieter offered Don five days in Dierks Studios.

The offer was surprising but certainly welcome, and Don readily agreed. "So I said, 'ok, I'll go to Germany. I got nothing else going on. My life is over, the band is screwed up, we're not playing anywhere and I was working on cars.' "34

With Don agreeing to another trip to Germany, the last vestige of the Dokken lineup quickly fell apart.

Arriving in Germany with no band, Don did some recording with the Scorpions. In an interview, the singer stated that he recorded scratch vocals (a vocal performance that a singer records to provide a reference track that music producers and audio engineers can use as they craft other pieces of the recorded song. It's primarily done for timing)

---

34 YouTube interview Don Dokken, we'll chain you up with a woman, (2 of 5).

for "No One Like You," "You Give Me All I Need," and "Dynamite." In the interview, Don stated, "I was just helping Klaus out, and you'll never hear those tracks because it's not fair to the Scorpions."[35]

Klaus eventually made a full recovery and returned to record the album which would turn out to be the chart killing *Blackout.*

While working with the Scorpions, Don was also looking for a record deal and recording demos with the help of Michael Wagener. Because Don had arrived in Germany with no band, Tom Croucier—brother of Juan Croucier— and Bobby Blotzer sat in on the demos. Tom and Bobby just happened to be in Germany working on an album with Vic Vergat at Dieter Dierks studio. "So, Bobby and Tom did the rhythm tracks," said Don, "and I cut, "Paris is Burning" and a couple of others, and that was that."[36]

After completing the demos, Don got the recording into the hands of Gaby Hauke, the manager for the band Accept, who had been recording in an adjacent studio.

"I probably should give her all the credit for my career," said Don. "She liked the demo and she said, 'I'm going to Hamburg to meet with Rolf Baierle the president of Carrere records. Let me play him your demo and see what he thinks.' She flies back two days later and I pick her up at the airport. And she says, 'he wants to give you a record deal,' and I said, 'you got to be kidding me.' And she's like, 'yep, $10,000 dollars.' And I said, '$10,000 dollars'—which is like a joke, but when you're broke $10,000 dollars is a lot of fucking money. I said, 'I'll take it.' So he signed me."

---

35 Wikipedia, Don Dokken.
36 Don Dokken interview with James Curl.

With a record deal in hand and his dreams of becoming a rock star within reach, Don flew back to L.A. in search of a new band.

Chapter 3
George and Mick

Having landed a European record deal, Don was excited, however he had one major problem—he didn't have a band. "So here's the dilemma," said Don. "I have a record deal but no band. So that's when I reached out to Mick and George Lynch."[37]

George Lynch was born September 28, 1954 in Spokane, Washington, but grew up in Los Angeles, California. Like most guitar prodigies, he began growing callouses on his fingers at an early age—in his case he started strumming at 10 but didn't get serious until he was about 13. "I had no idea what I was doing. I was more into posing with it than playing with it at first,"[38] said George.

Growing up in the '60s and early '70s, George was exposed to an abundance of great guitarists. His early influences included such renowned players as Jimi Hendrix, Jeff Beck, and Eric Clapton. "I had some earlier influences that my father turned me onto," said George. "He was sort of an audiophile, big music appreciator and we had a lot of music in our home, so I listened to a lot of jazz music and r&b."[39]

As a young boy, George would practice by putting on records and plugging his Teisco guitar into the console of his father's reel to reel stereo tape player. He discovered that by doing this he could distort the signal and send the guitar sound through the speakers. "I ended up blowing up his

---

37 Don Dokken interview with James Curl.
38 Dokken to Lynch Mob to Art, by Michelle Sathe, February 21, 2009.
39 You Tube interview, George Lynch, part 1 of 4.

stereo by doing that,"[40] said George. He would then play while watching his reflection in the window.

By the time George was attending Paramount high school he had gained the reputation as a hotshot guitarist. His skills eventually got him noticed by a couple of older guys who invited him to join their group and perform at a "battle of the bands." His leap from the bedroom to the stage, however, did little to give the impression that someday he would become a full-blown guitar hero.

Way out of his league and overcome with stage fright, the young guitarist froze in front of the audience which included friends and family members. Clumsily fumbling through the first song and unable to play, the curtains were dropped and George was escorted from the stage. After his disastrous performance he was promptly axed; embarrassed, yet undaunted he continued to play.

It was at this time that George formed a blues style rock band called Tungus Grump with some neighborhood friends. The guys were even forward thinking enough to have business cards made up with the band's name. Tungus Grump eventually became a popular band on the backyard party circuit and competed in several "battle of the bands" competitions. Being in Tungus Grump helped George progress as a player. The band also helped build his confidence during his formative years, particularly for playing live and gave the youngster a much needed creative outlet.

By the time he was 17, like most teenagers he began to rebel. He grew his hair long and spent all summer at the beach partying with his rowdy friends. Not agreeing with

---

40 You Tube interview, George Lynch, part 2 of 4.

their son's choice of lifestyle, George's parents thought a change of scenery might do the boy some good. In an attempt to reform him, they sent him to live with his godparents in Northern California—without his guitar.

A year later George returned home. Rusty and out of practice, he got busy thickening up his callouses and rededicated himself to the guitar. Shortly thereafter the Lynch family relocated to Auburn, California, a small town near Sacramento.

It was while living in Auburn that George answered an advertisement in the local newspaper for a band in need of a guitarist. As it turned out the guy who ran the ad was a boisterous kid with a shock of thick hair a quick laugh and a contagious smile named, "Wild" Mick Brown.

Remembering the incident, Mick said, "Well, I lived in Northern California, and I was still living at home. I think I was sixteen, I put an ad in the paper. I was playing with these guys, we were going to be a glitter rock band, or we were a glitter rock band, and we needed a guitar player. Well, he answered the ad and it turned out he lived very close to me, where my parents lived. He was seventeen, maybe eighteen; I think we're two years apart. And I became pretty serious. I mean, I was serious at a young age of wanting to chase this dream that I had, which I'm living now. He had never met anybody like that and thought, 'Wow, I have that in me but I never met anybody like you that wanted to go there.' I said, well, let's stay together and follow this through."[41]

Mick Brown was born on September 8, 1956 in San Mateo, California. The Browns eventually relocated and

---

41 "Wild" Mick Brown, *Glide Magazine*, December 30, 2013, by Leslie Michele Derrough.

settled in Meadow Vista, a small town near Auburn, California.

Recalling how he first got into music, Mick said, "When I was about five, I really thought I wanted to play music and I saw something on TV and I thought, 'Oh saxophone.' My parents looked at me like, 'You're only five, your fingers can't even.' Then as time went on, I think I was seven, and I thought, 'Oh guitar.' So, I went to take the guitar lesson and I found out my hands were much too small and it didn't seem right for me. Then I saw the Beatles on *Ed Sullivan* and I said, 'Oh wow, I could do the drum thing.' I thought that would be a safe bet. Instead of being in front of the screaming fans, I could be behind these drums, which I regretted later because I wanted to be in front. So on my eighth birthday, my parents go, 'If you're really serious about playing drums, would you learn how to do it, actually take lessons?'

"So, they took me on my eighth birthday to a guy named Mickey Hart, who two years later he was the drummer in the Grateful Dead. So, I did this in the South Bay area of San Francisco. I think it was called San Carlos and I went there and took drum lessons. On my tenth birthday, I think, I went there and the shop said, 'Closed, joined the Grateful Dead.' And I never saw him again."[42]

After becoming fast friends, George and Mick played for a while in a band called Sargent Rocks, which eventually evolved into Zoltar Galactic Gladiator of the Blue Skies and finally the Boyz. For a time they played around Auburn and the Sacramento area, but soon realized that they were going nowhere in a hurry. The two decided that if they were going

---

42 Ibid.

to have a shot at attaining their rock 'n' roll dreams there was only one place to be—Los Angeles and the Sunset Strip.

A short while later, Mick and George arrived in the City of Angels circa 1974 and rented a place to live in North Long Beach—a one-room studio on the bad side of town that was lacking a kitchen and had a bathroom with no shower.

Recalling the time, George said, "We lived off our girlfriends, who worked at Burger King. They fed us and let us take showers at their houses."[43]

Their living arrangements notwithstanding, the aspiring musicians found L.A to be an exciting place to live. Speaking about the Strip, Mick said, "It was the most fantastic thing. Ok. Christmas, your birthday, Easter, Thanksgiving, Columbus Day, Lincoln's Day, Washington, all in one. First off, drug abuse was huge and drugs were phenomenal. Oh my God, cocaine was the ticket. Not only were we doing cocaine, we were smoking pot, we were drinking, we were fucking—anything you could possibly do."[44]

Once Mick and George had settled in, they quickly got the Boyz up and running. They recruited bassist Monte Zufelt and vocalist Michael White. Michael had previously fronted the band London, which featured such notable members as Nikki Sixx, Blackie Lawless and Izzy Stradlin. Nikki would go on to play bass in Mötley Crüe, Blackie would form W.A.S.P and Izzy would play guitar for Guns N' Roses.

"My band played a hall party," said Michael, "they used to be called hall parties. You would rent a hall and then advertised with fliers and make all the money at the door. So,

---

43 Dokken to Lynch Mob to Art, by Michelle Sathe, February 21, 2009.
44 Ibid.

I played a hall party and the guy who was partnering with me on that said, 'you know there is this band called the Boyz looking for a singer and I think you would be a great fit.' And so he gave me their number and I called them.

"They had a rehearsal studio when I met them and we used to practice there all the time, pretty much every day. That would have been 1974, the end of '74. We played everywhere. We played Gazzaris, the Whisky a Go Go, the Starwood all the time. We played a lot of off the wall places. We played the Golden West Ball Room with Van Halen and with the Runaways a lot. We were the opening band for them.

"I went to high school at Long Beach Poly and at that time Lita Ford was actually going to school there too, so we knew each other. Basically, a year after I graduated in '73 I saw her playing around town and I told her I was in this band called the Boyz. And she said, 'yeah, our manager Kim Fowley is looking for another band.' So we were playing in Hollywood at the time and Rodney Bingenheimer (the famous disc jockey who was on the L.A. rock station KROQ) was a big fan of our band and I used to hang out with Rodney a bit. I told Rodney that Lita was a friend of mine and that Kim Fowley was her manager. So he got Kim to come and check us out and Kim liked us, so he started having us open for the Runaways. And we opened for them all over the place."[45]

Over time, the Boyz became a popular band on the Strip and gained a large following as well as the attention of some serious players.

"It was Halloween 1976," said Michael, "and it was Kiss everywhere and we were playing at Gazzaris and everybody was dressed up like Kiss; all the people who came there, I would say ninety percent painted their faces and they were dressed up like Kiss. And so we were on stage and we said,

---

45 Michael White interview with James Curl.

'let's do some Kiss.' So we played "Fire House" and we played "Detroit Rock City," and we played "Beer Drinker and Hell Raisers" and some other ZZ Top and we did some originals.

"And after the set was over we were packing up our stuff and everybody was going about their business. Nobody in the crowd was paying any attention to us and this guy comes walking up to me and says, 'Hi, I'm Gene Simmons,' and it was Gene Simmons. He didn't have his makeup on, but nobody knew what he looked like without his makeup, so he was perfectly incognito and he goes, 'I really like the way you did our songs.' And I'm looking at him and I didn't know if it was Gene Simons or not, but he was deadly serious.

"Then the guy that was with him handed me a card that said Casablanca Records and it had his manager's name on it and I thought, 'this is Gene Simmons.' And Gene said, 'Where you guys playing? I want to bring down the record company to check you out.' So I said, 'We're gonna be playing at the Starwood on Friday.' And he goes, 'I'll be there with the record company, put me on the guest list.' And I said, 'Absolutely!' and I introduced him to the band and everybody met him. So everybody was all excited, we're gonna be at the Starwood and it's gonna be amazing.

"So, we practiced every day until the show, and we were totally burned out; my voice was gone and we overdid it. You know, we were young and dumb. So we were playing at the Starwood that night with Van Halen and we would rotate sets. So we did the first set and there's Kiss, they come walking in right when we got on stage and they sat down upstairs and they had a whole posse.

"So, we did our set and we went backstage to our dressing rooms and they come in and Gene had Bebe Buell that famous groupie with him. And they're talking to us about doing demos and Gene really liked our set and everybody was all excited about it, and we talked and talked. Then Van Halen started their set and they all went out and saw Van Halen and then they went back to Van Halen's dressing room and did the same thing with them, and they flew them back to New York and did demos. So we were very, very close to getting to go back to New York to do demos, but Van Halen was better, they were the better band and the rest is history."[46]

The incident of which Michael is referring to is of course, the famous Gene Simmons demo tapes. Gene flew Van Halen to New York, financed and produced the demos and then presented them to his managers. After hearing the demos, their response was that Van Halen had, "no chance of making it" and they "wouldn't take them." In what turned out to be a monumental mistake, Gene then opted out. A year-and-a-half later Van Halen was signed by Warner Bros. and became one of the biggest bands in the world.

"That was in '76," continued Michael, "and we stayed together until '77. Sometime in '77 was when I left the band."[47]

After Michael left the Boyz, vocalist Greg Sanford was brought in and the guys elected to change the band's name to Xciter. Over the next year-and-a-half the quartet played all the L.A. hot spots and gained a large fan base with their Van Halen esque sound. They also recorded a couple of promising demos and came close to being signed, but destiny had other plans.

Unable to secure a record deal, the guys became frustrated and Greg eventually left. At this time the musical landscape had changed and the popularity of New Wave was on the

<hr>

[46] Michael White interview with James Curl.
[47] Ibid.

rise. Trying to adapt, the guys decided to bring in singer Lisa Furspanker, and completely change their image.

The new lineup and look did little to re-energize the band and it seemed as if George and Mick would never get their big break. But destiny, as it often does, was about to change all that. Don Dokken, having just come back from Germany, was looking to put a band together and George and Mick were on his radar.

Don had known Mick and George for a number of years, having played with them all over the Strip when they were known as the Boyz. In fact, Don had first met George and Mick at the Smoke Stack in Redondo Beach when his band Airborn opened for the Boyz. Don had also used two songs that George and Mick had written, "Paris is Burning" and "In the Middle" as part of the demo that secured him a record deal.

Speaking of how Don got the songs, Mick said, "He took some material that George and I had wrote, and took it to Germany and pretty much put his name on it, you know what I am saying (laughing) and he got a recording contract. So he called me up to play. I looked over at George and I said, 'George, this guy's got our music and he's got a record deal' and we were pretty upset about that because he's got our songs. But then we also thought, it's kind of an open door, so we went along with it. I think probably when people talk about the turmoil in Dokken, that was pretty much the moment where it all started. I remember Don asking us if he could take some of our songs over there to try and get something going in Europe and we said 'No' but he did anyway."[48]

---

48 Destroyer of Harmony, George Lynch and Don Dokken, January 4, 2015.

"Don said he had an interest in recording one of my songs," said George speaking of the incident. "He had a publishing deal in Europe. I said, 'I'm listening.' So next think you know, he's asking to come by and hear my material and do a deal. He wanted to record it for some money. I said 'cool.' But he never called me back or showed up.

"He went to Europe and sold the song, but didn't put our names on it. He put his name on it, made money and spent it. He came back to America and asked for me to form a band with him. During this conversation, I brought up the song issue. I asked to see the paperwork on the publishing deal. He was very nervous about it. In the back pages (of the contract) was a signatory page with his signature on it. It said, "Paris Is Burning" written by Don Dokken."[49]

When asked years later why he didn't sue Don, Lynch explained, "When Don rips someone off, he covers his ass. He really docs. That's exactly what happened." Lynch also said he didn't have enough to get a lawyer at the time and also, suing in Europe would have proved too much of a hassle, "...but what was I going to do, pay in Deutsche marks?! I drove a liquor truck, so I didn't make enough money to hire a lawyer. On the one hand, you can sue; on the other, you can join his (Don's) band."

Having been away in Germany, it had been several months since Don had seen the two. Needless to say he was surprised by what he found.

"So, I called them up," explained Don, "and they weren't doing anything. Same problem, Rock was out, New Wave was in." By this time, however, the Xciter that Don knew had

---

49 *BraveWords*, George Lynch claims Don Dokken burned him over "Paris is Burning" track.

changed. "So, I go to see them," said Don, "they cut all their hair off, they have a girl singer and they're wearing sharkskin coats and pointy boots—they had completely gone New Wave. And I said, 'You gotta be kidding me.' "[50]

At first, Don only wanted to get Mick involved. He explained that he had gotten a deal with Carrere Records, a French label, and needed to put a band together. Mick was interested but only if George was included. But there was one problem. After the first meeting between Don and George it was obvious that neither thought much of the other.

George, who admitted to initially being a little suspicious of Don said, "He seemed kind of weird. A little sleazy."[51]

Don's first impression of George was hardly better. "I knew from the first day that I met him that something wasn't right," said Don. "I went to Mick and said that George seemed a little off, a little strange, he just seemed very angry."[52] Personality conflict notwithstanding, destiny had taken over and inexorable events had been set into motion.

"Mick grew up with George in high school," explained Don, "and he said, 'I really want to stay with George.' I didn't really want George in the band. But I realized that George was an amazing guitar player. And I thought, 'well, he's a lot better guitar player than I am.' So I took him."[53]

Don then offered both of them the opportunity to go to Germany and record an album, with the promise of $2,000 each. Having had a number of close calls with fame playing with the Boyz and Xciter, Mick and George were ready to try something different. "It was the chance to do a record," said George, "so of course we're gonna take that."[54]

---

50 Don Dokken interview with James Curl.
51 Dokken, the hair metal band that hated itself, by Paul Elliot, October 2, 2015.
52 *BlabberMouth.net*, Don Dokken: George Lynch didn't give a fuck about the fans, August 19, 2002.
53 Don Dokken interview with James Curl.
54 Dokken, the hair metal band that hated itself, by Paul Elliot, October 2, 2015.

Having recruited George and Mick into his band, big things were about to happen and the timing couldn't have been better. On a global level, the popularity of hard rock and heavy metal was about to skyrocket, and the Sunset Strip was leading the charge.

Chapter 4
Breaking the Chains
and Jeff Pilson

With George and Mick agreeing to go to Germany, Don once again planned on having Juan handle bass duties, but Juan's girlfriend had different ideas. "Juan was supposed to come over," said Don, "but Juan's girlfriend ends up being trippy, tears up his plane ticket and his passport and threw his bass out the apartment window, upstairs, three days before we left. And she said she had a revelation that Juan would die in a plane crash. So we had no bass player, Juan was out."[55]

With no time to find a replacement, Don, Mick and George left for Germany in July of 1981. Speaking of the time, George said, "Don had made a lot of promises, said he was best friends with the Scorpions and we're gonna have this huge rehearsal facility in Frankfurt with all these walls of Marshalls.

"So, we get over there and of course we didn't even have a flight, we had to kinda fake our way onto a charter flight and get all our equipment on there. Got us to Iceland, then we found our way to Amsterdam and from Amsterdam we hitched rides to Germany. We get to Germany and we have no place to live—all of us except Don, he always took care of himself. He had these people he knew to stay with, but we had to sort of fend for ourselves. So we lived at one point in a bomb shelter, an old German bomb shelter, where everything got mildewed and rotted.

---

55 Don Dokken interview with James Curl.

"The worst spot we stayed in was Hamburg, we were in Hamburg for some months and we stayed at this immigrant's hotel for refugees. And we were way at the top like in the attic and it was one room and there was a shower right in the middle of the room. And we all shared the one room and you had to shower in front of all the other guys. We didn't have a TV so that was our entertainment, watching each other shower. It was humble beginnings."[56]

Eventually by late July, the guys found their way into Dierks Studios in Stommeln, Germany. It was here that they also found a replacement for Juan. "Peter Baltes said, 'I'll play the bass tracks for 500 bucks,' " said Don. "So, Peter actually did the whole album."[57]

"It was down in the basement at Dierk's studio in Germany," said Lynch. "The Scorpions were upstairs. Rory Gallagher was upstairs. These guys wanted to hear what was going on, so they would bring down the guitar player from Scorpions and Rory. They would sit there. I was so proud of my guitar tracks. Me and Michael Wagener were holed up there. We'd board the place up. We wouldn't let anybody in. I had a 24-track tube machine and an MC500 board. I had one of Ritchie Blackmore's old cabinets and a Rangemaster treble booster and my Tiger guitar. It sounded so good. It was the first record I'd ever done, really, so we were committed to making a statement."[58]

It was while recording the album that the animosity between George and Don started to show and their legendary feud began to spark. "The problem was, George and I never

---

56 You Tube interview, George Lynch (2 of 4).
57 Don Dokken interview with James Curl.
58 You Tube interview, George Lynch (2 of 4).

got along from the very beginning. Every day was a struggle just trying to get something on tape with George."[59]

The problems actually started just as the guys were getting ready to begin work on the album. George approached Don and said that he and Mick wanted to go back to L.A. "He said Mick and I want to go home," explained Don. "We don't want to do this. And I'm like, well, we're starting the album tomorrow. My crew had been over, the record company would have dropped me, the whole *Breakin the Chains* almost didn't happen.

"The next day I was there, rehearsing in the cellar of a little hotel called Hotel Trost, in a wine cellar, and George said he didn't want to do it. And Dieter Dierks ended up talking to George and saying, 'Listen, Don's here, you should do this album, it's good for your career, it's only taking 15 days out of your life, you're going to get paid, and then you can go back to L.A. after two weeks.' And George said, 'I don't like it here, I don't like Don, I don't like his music, I don't want to do this.' And Dieter talked him into staying. From the day when we all started recording *Breakin the Chains*, my career almost didn't happen. George could have ended my career in one fell swoop. I could have phoned my record company and said, 'You just spent $5,000 in rehearsal time buying these two guys I hired for the band, and now they are going to bail on me.' I mean, this is how the band started with George. He was like that."[60]

From there, work on the album got underway, but Don and George continued to butt heads during the recording.

---

59 Don Dokken talks early days, acoustic shows and much more, by John Parks, December 7, 2012.
60 Ye Old Metal, Dokken's Tooth and Nail, by Martin Popoff.

Michael Wagener, who was there working with the guys said, "I wouldn't call it a feud. It was two big egos in the same room. Everybody had their ego and everybody wanted to punch their opinion through. But I didn't even take it that serious. But that created a little bit of tension and that came out in the music that they did and I thought that it was actually pretty good."[61]

Despite the difficulties between Don and George, by September *Breakin' the Chains* was completed. The album hit the market a few months later and did well on the charts of the British heavy metal magazine *Kerrang*.

Having completed the album, George and Mick returned to L.A. Don, who had a girlfriend in Germany, wound up staying for several more weeks, eventually returning to America sometime in late 1981.

By now things were really beginning to heat up on the Strip and the burgeoning Metal movement was starting to erupt. Mötley Crüe had debuted at the Starwood, opening for Y&T on April 24 and 25 of '81. From there the glam and hair metal era kicked into high gear, and the Strip would never be the same. Bands like Quiet Riot, Ratt and W.A.S.P were gaining lots of attention and getting major record deals.

Once home, Don regrouped with Mick, George and Juan and they showcased a couple of shows at the Roxy with Mötley Crüe. In attendance were representatives from several different record companies. "Mötley got signed, we didn't," said Don. Dejected after failing to secure the much sought after American record deal, the band split up. "George went his way," said Don, "Mick went his way, Juan

---

61 Michael Wagener interview with James Curl, November 1, 2018.

joined Ratt and that was it. And I was kinda just sitting there going, 'well I got a record, no band, I got nothing.' "[62]

It was then that Rolf Baierle informed Don that he could get Dokken another German tour slated for January of '82. "The record company said we can get you a tour in Germany," said Don, "and we will get you on the biggest TV show in Germany called the Beat-Club. Everybody from AC/DC to Led Zeppelin to Journey to David Bowie played the Beat-Club. It will be a one hour special on TV broadcast all over."[63]

Excited with the prospect of being on the Beat-Club, Don quickly regrouped with Mick, George and Juan. After rehearsing for a few weeks, the guys headed back to Germany. "So we did the tour," said Don, "eight shows, played the Beat-Club. We came home and George and Juan were just not getting along. So Juan quit and went back to Ratt."[64]

Several weeks later, on March 19, the tragic news that guitarist Randy Rhodes had been killed in an airplane accident shook the rock 'n' roll world.

Following Randy's passing, Ozzy Osbourne began looking for a suitable replacement. George, who was not ready to committing himself to Dokken just yet, headed over to Europe to try his luck auditioning for Randy's spot. As fate would have it, George would wind up losing out to Jake E. Lee.

Remembering the experience, George said, "I was very devastated. My wife was with me, I had quit my job. We had

---

62 Don Dokken interview with James Curl.
63 Ibid.
64 Ibid.

two little kids, we lived in an apartment. We didn't really have much money, so it was a great opportunity for me. I was a delivery driver for a liquor company and I would kind of deliver booze into the not-so-great areas. Nobody else wanted to drive into those areas so I took the job. It was a good union job so I made enough money to support us. And I had to quit the job to go do the Ozzy thing.

"And when they fired me like that… And they didn't pay me, and they didn't give me any compensation, they didn't ask me if I was okay or anything. They must have didn't care, they just said… It was literally like… It took, like a minute. Ozzy just said, 'Hey, it's not gonna work out. Thanks a lot for your time. See ya later. Bye.' Yeah, my jaw dropped. I couldn't believe it. My heart just dropped and… Yeah, I think I cried on the way home. It was very devastating."[65]

It wasn't the first time that George had auditioned for a spot in Ozzy's band. Back in 1979, George went up against Randy Rhodes, but came out on the losing end. There was no shame in the loss, however, as George got to take over as teacher for Randy's students. "Yeah, I got the consolation prize," said George. "We were both up for the gig, and obviously he got it, and I got his teaching job."[66]

While George was in Europe auditioning for Ozzy, Don and Mick were committed to putting together a stable line-up and started looking for top quality musicians. For a time, Dokken played shows with guitar wiz Warren DeMartini, and Juan on bass, but the lineup quickly fell apart after the band failed yet again to secure an American record deal. Juan

---

65 *BraveWords*, George Lynch talks about auditioning for Ozzy Osbourne's band, March 1, 2019.
66 *BraveWords*, interview George Lynch, March 10, 2015.

and Warren headed over to the Ratt camp, leaving Don and Mick wondering what they were going to do.

A short time later Don was unexpectedly contacted by Cliff Burnstein, from Q Prime management. While looking through a bin of import albums, Cliff had discovered a copy of *Breakin' the Chains* in a record store in Hoboken, New Jersey. Asking around, Cliff learned that Dokken was unsigned, at least in America, and were without a proper manager. Cliff, who really liked the record, eventually got in touch with Don and the two met in L.A. After their initial meeting, Don agreed to a deal that allowed Q Prime to become Dokken's manager.

To get the band some needed exposure, Cliff booked Dokken a showcase at the Roxy as the opener for Mötley Crüe. Needing a guitarist and a bass player, Don asked George and Juan if they would step in for the show, which they agreed to do. Following the gig, Cliff began negotiations to broker a deal with Elektra and get Dokken under contract.

"After the showcase we were signed and dropped three times on Elektra because of changes at the label," said Don. "At that time, Tom Zutaut was just working in the singles department, he believed in the record and kept pushing for us as well as Cliff. Eventually, we were offered a last chance showcase and landed a deal."[67]

Now represented by a major American label, and a big-time manager, Dokken was offered a tour as the warm-up act for Blue Oyster Cult and Aldo Nova. The future looked bright, however Juan had to get back to Ratt—their first

---

67 Dokken main man Don Dokken explains feud with George Lynch: "In the end we did some great records together," by Deb Rao, June 18, 2011.

official album *Ratt* had just been released and was starting to take off. As for George, he was still uncertain if he wanted to remain in Dokken, so for the moment he was out.

The next thing Q Prime focused on was to get *Breakin' the Chains* released in America. Work began on refining the album at Total Access Studio with the help of Michael Wagener who was once again living in L.A. In all, the album was remixed, partially re-recorded and renamed *Breaking the Chains*, as opposed to the German title, *Breakin' the Chains*.

There was one person however who felt that the album had already been altered enough—George Lynch. "I did like it when we originally recorded it, but then Don got ahold of it and destroyed it. He basically sent us home from Europe and said, 'OK, guys, we're done. I'm just going to stay back and hang out with my girlfriend.' I was thinking, 'OK.' What he did was he stayed in the studio when we were gone and had his way with the record, which was to pump up all the vocals, take all my guitars out. Destroy the mix. It just sounded weak and wimpy. It just killed it. It was actually pretty muscular and pretty tough when we were in the studio. Quite honestly, the sound was just unbelievable. Then when it was all done, he did what he did to it and he killed it. It's very hard for me to listen to because of that, because I knew what it was and nobody will ever hear that unfortunately."[68]

The newly polished album hit the American market in September of '83. Fan reaction was lukewarm and it only managed to reach 136 on the *Billboard* 200. While not a hit album, the LP did contain a couple of standout tunes, "Paris is Burning" and "Breaking the Chains." Even Don admitted that it was not a great album. "There were some vapid, bad

---

68 Don Dokken and George Lynch dispute *Breaking the Chains,* January 6, 2015.

attempts to write a hit song," said Don. "I tried and failed miserably."[69]

With the record released and a tour scheduled, plans to get a video on MTV (that's "music television" for the younger readers) quickly got underway. The band, though, was still lacking a permanent bass player.

"I called Mike Varney and he recommended Jeff Pilson who was playing in a top forty band in a bar with Amy Cannon who eventually became one of the background singers in Mötley Crüe."[70]

A few days later Don gave Jeff a call and set up a time to meet. Remembering the events that led up to his first meeting with Don, Jeff said, "I moved to L.A in the spring of '83. I was living in the Bay area and the rock scene had died a horrible death, there was just no rock scene. The punk thing had happened there and it was all Punk and New Wave. It just was not my scene at all, I just felt musically out of place even though I loved the Bay area. I just wanted to rock, I was ready to rock. And I'd heard about this Metal thing in L.A. Actually to be honest, I didn't know much about the Metal thing in L.A until I got there. I joined a cover band to get to L.A., kinda the first thing I could find in order to get in and I found a band that was making a decent living, they were good people and they were a pretty good band.

"So, I got there and did that. Shortly after that I formed a band with my good friend Mark Nelson and Paul Horowitz, who later became Paul Taylor of Winger fame. And we had

---

69 Dokken, the hair metal band that hated itself, by Paul Elliot, October 2, 2015.
70 Dokken main man Don Dokken explains feud with George Lynch: "In the end we did some great records together," by Deb Rao, June 18, 2011.

a top forty cover band that played clubs and was an amazing band, really, really amazing and that was really fun.

"But then that's when the call came from Don Dokken, because Don had called Mike Varney, the infamous connector of people and all that. Don called him and said, 'Hey, I'd like to find a singing bass player.' And Mike said, 'Hey, I know a guy who just moved to L.A and is a singing bass player.'

"So, Mike called me and said, 'Would you like to do this?' and I said God, yes. They had a record deal. It sounded like, wow, this is cool. So, Don called me and I went to his house and met him and heard the music, and just kind of got to know him. Then we went out to the Rainbow and the Troubadour to see Great White.

"It was just so exciting because there were all these rock bands playing out and there was a rock scene and there were girls, it was rocker's paradise, it really was. All I can say is it was so much fun. And once I joined the band I started really getting in with a bunch of the people. You know, it got a little crazy, the partying and stuff got out of hand, but it was a part of youth that I still kinda cherish.

"So, then we arranged an audition so I could play. We played for about 20 minutes, the power in the house blew up. And as soon as the power blew up Don said, 'So you wanna join the band?' And I said of course, yes. And, so I did and I was in the band."[71]

Recalling the events, Don said, "At first Jeff was hesitant. He really didn't want to join the band because he wanted to be a lead singer and start his own band. I asked Jeff if he wanted to join the band and go on tour and he said, 'I don't

---

71 Jeff Pilson interview with James Curl.

know, I got this really good gig.' And I said, 'wait a minute, you want to pass on the Blue Oyster Cult tour and making the Breaking the Chains video?' So he joined the band and we went on tour with Blue Oyster Cult."[72]

With Jeff in the band, the multi-talented bass player quickly became an indispensable member. Not only did he prove himself a great musician, he showed that he was a competent songwriter and had a great singing voice as well. In fact, he would co-write some of Dokken's biggest chart toppers and help create the unique sound that would become unmistakably Dokken.

Born in Lake Forest, Illinois on January 19, 1959 Jeffrey Steven Pilson showed a propensity for music at an early age. "Well, I was 12 when I started playing. A friend of mine and I used to sing this TV commercial that was on at the time, this was in Milwaukee, Wisconsin. Some guys heard me doing it on the schoolyard and so they said, 'we're starting a band, we want you to sing, but we don't have a bass player, would you play bass?' I said, 'sure, why not?' So, I had a paper route at the time and I went out and bought a Teisco Del Ray bass and a Gibson Skylark amp, for $35 bucks each. And I started learning how to play. And of course that band never happened, but it actually got me started on bass, which is kinda cool.[73]

"Then a year later, when I was 13, I ended up moving to the state of Washington to a very small mill town in Southwest Washington, where the schools were quite far behind. The whole town was kinda geared for people going into the mill right from high school, so the education was not

---

72 Don Dokken interview with James Curl.
73 Jeff Pilson interview with James Curl.

that great and my eighth grade year scholastically was a complete repeat of seventh grade.

"So very quickly I got in with some guys who could kind of play, you know some musicians, sort of you know kid musicians, but I thought they were good at the time; they were better than me at that time. So I got in with them and started doing drugs and everything else and all the other stuff you do when you're 14 years old and just starting to play music.

"Moving to that town got me very serious because I felt very out of place there. They were into hunting and fishing which I had never done, so I was kind of a fish out of water. You know I had come from the sixth rated school district in the country in Whitefish Bay, Wisconsin to whatever number it was—it was not number six that's for sure. So, like I say you know that's when the whole idea of growing your hair and doing drugs and playing music kinda took over my life."[74]

Over the course of the ensuing years Jeff not only learned to play the bass, he also became proficient with the guitar, cello, keyboards, piano, and mellotron.

With Jeff on bass and Mick behind the kit, Don figured he would once again take up the responsibility of both vocals and guitar. However, with a video coming up and a tour scheduled, Dokken's management convinced Don to bring Lynch in. It took some persuading, but Don eventually agreed.

With Lynch as an official member, the "classic line up" was finally assembled. The guys filmed their first video for the song "Breaking the Chains," which promptly found a

---

74 Ibid

home on MTV, and then readied themselves for their first "big" tour.

"It all sounded great," said Don, "I was excited we would be playing in arenas but had reservations about George. We had never got along even when making *Breakin' the Chains*.

"I was still playing guitar at the time but George was obviously a great guitarist. We did a quick low budget video and as you'll see in the video I was still playing guitar. It was a two-guitar band until *Tooth and Nail*. I was then asked to become just the frontman, which was hard, I had always played guitar and sang, so it was a hard transition to stop playing. But it gave George more freedom to become the great guitarist he turned out to be."[75]

Before heading out on the tour, fate intervened. It was around this time that Don became acquainted with Jack Russell through his friendship with Gary Holland. Because of this, Don would also discover one of the bigger bands to come out of the '80s—Great White.

"Gary called me and said, 'I got this new band, can you come and check us out and help us out with a demo?' So I went out to this garage, you know the typical garage with carpet on the walls made into a rehearsal studio. And at the time they were called Dante Fox."[76]

"So, Don came down with Garry Holland to the garage where we rehearsed," said Jack "and Gary introduced me to Don and he like the band and me and Don just hit it off."[77]

"So I went and saw them play," recalled Don, "and said, 'yeah, you guys are really good, you just need some direction, your songs are kind of a mess and you need some production.' So Michael Wagener and I took them into the studio and for $7,500 dollars we recorded the demo *Out of the Night* (a five song EP). So, yeah, I basically discovered

---

75 Ibid.
76 Don Dokken interview with James Curl.
77 Jack Russell interview with James Curl.

them in a garage, took them into a studio, made the EP and got them a record deal."[78]

Giving his own recollection of how things happened Jack said, "Then Don came to see us play at the Whisky and he brought this guy named Allen Niven who worked for Enigma records. And he came down and Allen hated the band, fucking hated it; granted we had a really bad night. We had a bass player that used to hack his bass up with a pick axe, he had a cheese grater on the back of his bass and would slice his fingers all up and throw blood on the audience. And we were like, oh my god, really dude. All we did was ask you to move around a little bit. But this guy takes it to the extreme. He wears chains around his neck, but they were like the Queen Mary anchor chains; talk about taking something to the extreme. So Allen didn't like the band, but Don said, 'come on and see them again.' So he came down and saw us again. And we gave him some demo tapes and he decided that he wanted to sign us."[79]

Subsequently, after being signed the guys changed their name to Great White, a name Don may very well have had a hand in coming up with.

"There are many stories of how it came about," said Don. "Their manager claims responsibility for doing it, that's all bullshit. Mark (the guitar player) is very tall and blond hair and very pale skin and he's a big guy like 6' 3" and my nickname for him was 'Great White;' I always called Mark 'Great White.' And somehow that name and because Jack's an avid fisherman, somehow they came up with that name. I won't take credit for it."[80]

---

78 Don Dokken interview with James Curl.
79 Jack Russell interview with James Curl.
80 Don Dokken interview with James Curl.

With a new name, a fresh demo and Allan Niven as their manager, things started to move quickly for Great White. Being ambitious Allan convinced the L.A. radio station KMET and its neighboring station KLOS to put a couple of the demo's tracks on heavy rotation. Because of the consistent radio play Great White began drawing thousands of people to their shows instead of hundreds. This forced the band to move from local clubs to larger venues like the Perkins Palace in Pasadena and The Palace in Hollywood. Due to their increase in popularity Great White were able to headline a show at Six Flags Magic Mountain in Valencia playing to 6,250, as an unsigned act. In late 1983 EMI Records took notice and promptly signed the band. A few months later, in early 1984, they would release their debut album *Great White*.

Having become fast friends it was around this time that Jack moved into Don's place for a time. Commenting on a few memories Jack said, "George and Mick called me up, I was living with Don and they called me up. I'm not sure if Jeff was on the line or not, but they called me up and they wanted to kick Don out and have me sing and I'm like, 'Dude, the band is called Dokken.' And I said, 'You realize you're calling me at his house and Don is a really good friend of mine. You think when we hang up I'm not going to tell him that this phone call happened?' I said, 'Look, I appreciate the acknowledgement and all that good stuff, but I'm already in a band which I love and second of all I would never do that to my friend.'

"There are some things where you gotta draw the line somewhere and if that's how I'm gonna make it in this business, then I ain't gonna make it in this business. I guess I have too big of a heart or something. I told Don, but I don't know what happened after that, I didn't ask.

"The fact of the matter is Don is a great songwriter, we've written songs together. I call him dad, he calls me son. We've always had a really unique relationship and he's always been there to help me out when I need help, and ya know I'll always be there for him."[81]

Jack went on to say, "Don was instrumental, I mean everything. He produced the first record, he produced the first EP, he co-wrote songs. Ya know he just took his time, which he didn't have to do, and invested it in us. And he was like the proud dad.

"I just can't say enough good things about him. People talk shit about him, ya know. I remember one night I was at his house, it was a New Year's Eve party and the singer for a band called Malice was there. And we were sitting there inside the house and we're drinking and he's just talkin' shit about Don. And we're sitting there drinking and I'm thinking, 'this motherfucker is drinking Don's booze in Don's house, talking shit about Don.' So I go, 'hey, let's go outside and have a smoke, man.' And he said 'all right.'

"So we went outside and I beat the living shit out of him. I'm talking the last I remember he was in the middle of the street and I had my hands clasped together and I was smashing his face. And Bobby Blotzer was yelling, 'Let him go, dude! Just let him go! And they pulled me off of him. And we get him into Blotzer's house, which was a duplex that we shared. And Bobby comes out and says, 'goddam it, Jack, he's bleeding all over my carpet you fucking asshole!' So they had to take him to the hospital."[82]

With Great White set on a path to rock 'n' roll stardom, Dokken headed out on tour in December of '83. For three months they played warm-up for Blue Oyster Cult and Aldo Nova and got a taste of what it was like playing the big

---

81 Jack Russell interview with James Curl.
82 Ibid

venues. In March they returned home to L.A., but despite a successful outing the news from Cliff Burnstein wasn't good.

"We came home," said Don, "and he said, 'yeah, it was great, you sold a hundred thousand records, you only owe the record company a half a million dollars.' " Flabbergasted at the news, the guys were understandably disappointed. "Here I had just done an arena tour for three months and we were absolutely broke, not only were we broke but we were massively in debt,"[83] said Don.

And if that wasn't bad enough, Dokken's record label, Elektra, was threatening to drop them. Elektra felt that Dokken hadn't lived up to expectations and that *Breaking the Chains* was a failure.

Speaking of the incident, Don said, "The record company said, 'We don't like the band, they're not going anywhere, we gave them a push, it's over.' The label wanted to drop us because we only sold 100,000 copies of *Breaking the Chains* originally. They're like, 'you're not worth it, other bands are selling millions.'

"So I begged on my hands and knees for the label to give us one more chance. Our managers had to beg them to keep us on the label." It took some convincing but eventually the Elektra executives relented. "They said, 'We'll give you one more shot,' " said Don. "So we were up against the wall. So, that's why we came up with the title *Tooth and Nail*. If we're going to make it, it's going to be with a fight."[84]

---

83 You Tube interview Don Dokken, *Tooth and Nail*, (3 of 5).
84 Wikipedia, Don Dokken.

Chapter 5
Tooth and Nail

With *Breaking the Chains* being considered a dud by their record label, Dokken now found themselves in a precarious situation. They knew that second chances didn't come around very often and if their next album didn't deliver "big time," the game would be over.

As if their less than auspicious start wasn't enough, the guys were barely scraping by. Their management was only giving them $200 each, per week, to live on. As a result, their dietary intake sank to an all-time low, while their consumption of Top Ramen and hot dogs rose to new heights.

"On the good days, on Sundays," said Don, "we would have the big bowl of Top Ramen boiling. And someone would bring over some hot dogs and we would chop them up and throw them in. We lived on Top Ramen, that's reality, Top Ramen, every musician has lived on Top Ramen."[85]

To help supplement their meager income, George and Mick were driving liquor delivery trucks for the Gallows Wine Company. "At one point," said George, "I was a liquor delivery driver in South Central L.A. I did the routes no one would take because they were in such dangerous parts of town. My route was Martin Luther King Boulevard. In fact, on the day I signed my record deal, I was in my liquor van, and I had to drive to the Elektra building in L.A. and sign the contract, and then I went right back on my route."[86]

---

85 YouTube interview, Living Legends Music interview with Don Dokken, *Tooth and Nail* (3 of 5) July 21, 2008.
86 Welcome to the Jungle: The definitive oral history of 80's metal, Jon Wiederhorn, May 22, 2013.

With the guys roughing it out they were determined to write a great album. Ironically, the hard times probably helped Dokken more than it hindered them. Their desperate situation pulled from them the greatness that was within each of them, both individually and collectively. It also showed just how "hungry" they were. "What good came out of that?" said Don. "We wrote *Tooth and Nail*. Every song was like this is it, boys, it's make it or break it. If this album doesn't go, it's over."[87]

Speaking of the writing process for *Tooth and Nail,* Jeff said, "When we were on the road during the Breaking the Chains tour, which was our first tour together, George and I would often room together and we would generally bring little amps and guitars and a bass into the room and we would jam. We had a little portable recorder and we recorded a bunch of ideas on the road."[88]

Back home, George and Jeff took their song ideas and began refining and recording them on a four-track recorder at George's place. "Then when we got home, I spent about a month practically living at George's house and Mick was living there at the time. George and I would basically work all day and write and Mick would come home from the bar at one or two in the morning and he would have fresh ideas. So we would then do more work. And Mick contributed some important stuff that way. So after that month we had a real strong basis of material."[89]

Although Don didn't participate in the writing sessions at George's house, he was hard at work at his place, oftentimes with Jeff at his side.

---

87 YouTube interview, Living Legends Music interview with Don Dokken, *Tooth and Nai*l (3 of 5) July 21, 2008.
88 Jeff Pilson interview with James Curl.
89 Ye Olde Metal, Dokken's Tooth and Nail, by Martin Popoff.

"What you have to understand," said Jeff, "is, so much of it was done distantly. There was very little communication going on. I mean, the writing sessions for *Tooth and Nail* were really fun, but they were funny.

"Then I also spent some time working with Don. He and I wrote "Alone Again," and it was from an old song that he had, and we reworked that, and felt really good about that, although nobody else did at the time. And "Into the Fire," he and I were working on it, and like I say, it was actually a finished song, and then we got the studio and George changed the chorus for way better. And so he spent a lot of time on that, on those two things. And then the only other thing he did was we had a song called "Bullets to Spare." George and I had the music, but we basically never came up with anything vocally for our song. And we didn't care for the music Don had for his "Bullets to Spare," so he just threw his vocals on our "Bullets to Spare"—his lyrics basically got used on our music for that song. And other than that, I think that's pretty much all he did on that record."[90]

Continuing, Jeff went on to say, "The whole *Tooth and Nail* writing process and tour was magical for me. I was new in the band and instantly established a bond with George as we spent a lot of time working on the album. It's a lifelong bond. The band was really hungry and there was a healthy competition. It was a positive experience all around."[91]

After a month of concentrated work the guys had composed about 25 songs. From there they trimmed it down to the 10 best. When they got to the ballad "Alone Again," George voiced his strong objection to the song, saying that the album shouldn't contain any ballads. "Ballads are for

90 Ibid.
91 *BraveWords*, bassist Jeff Pilson talks band's break up, August 29, 2016

pussies," said the guitarist. He was however out voted, and as time would show, thankfully so.

With their best songs assembled the guys headed into the studio. Recording and sequencing the album took place at L.A.'s well-renowned Cherokee studio between April and August of '84. Right from the get-go recording the album was fraught with difficulties. Don suggested using his friend Michael Wagener, who had produced *Breaking the Chains*. The rest of the band however didn't agree with Don's pick. They felt that Michael and Don were in cahoots and that together they would try and make the album all about Don, i.e. turning up the vocals.

To try and alleviate the disagreement, Elektra brought in the capable Tom Werman, who had worked with the likes of Cheap Trick, Molly Hatchet, Ted Nugent and Mötley Crüe. Bringing in Tom, however, created a slew of other problems between him and Geoff Workman the engineer.

Recalling his experience working with Dokken, Tom said, "The engineer Geoff Workman whom I had worked with on *Shout at the Devil,* he was a very evil and divisive guy, he had major issues but he was a brilliant engineer. What he did typically with his projects was to pick out one of the band members that he was influential with and try to alienate them from the producer. He would try and convince the band that he, the engineer, was the genius behind all this and without him the project would fall apart, and that the producer didn't know what he was doing. He did a number of things to distance George. He would run me down to George all the time. He went so far as to record my voice and edit various conversations together to make me say things that I never said."[92]

---

92 Tom Werman interview with James Curl.

One of the edits that Geoff put together made Tom seem as if he were homosexual and wanted to give everyone in the band a blow job. The tape was played for George and from then on George was suspicious of Tom's sexual orientation. The tapes would go on to be known as the infamous "head tapes."

"It was so ridiculous that I was amazed that George actually believed it," remarked Tom.

Because of the suspicion created by the tapes, George developed a dislike of Tom, and the two eventually had a big blowout. Things finally erupted when George adamantly refused advice from Werman concerning some of his solos; the guitarist then stubbornly refused to work with Tom any longer.

"What happened was he was doing a solo on a song and he had already done the song "Tooth and Nail," which has a remarkable guitar solo, one of the best I ever heard. I thought George was brilliant, he is brilliant. I mean even Zakk Wylde's solo in the movie Rock Star, on one of those songs, even that, I didn't think was up to George's "Tooth and Nail" solo. I said, 'George, this is great this solo, what you're doing you're playing very fast, you're shredding and it's very impressive, but I don't hear any real melody that I can remember or grab. It would be great if you could come up with something like your solo on "Tooth and Nail" that goes from point A to point B. That solo was a real journey, a nice composition and this is just piddling around.' And he lost it and he said, 'I'm not playing! Get the fuck out of here!' He pitched a fit. And I said, 'Wow, you're really angry. Would you perhaps feel better by hitting me?' And I kinda invited him to take it out on me and he backed off.

"But I said I can't work like this. And I had done, I don't know, maybe four fifths of the album by that time. I called the manager that day and I worked out a deal so that I would get a settlement and I would leave and they would get somebody else and they got Michael and Roy Thomas Baker, both of whom were great, you know. And I think they did a really great job finishing the album. Michael did a good job mixing the album and that was it.

"I got along very well with Don, Jeff and Mick, they were fine. Of course, George and Don hated each other. George was a hot-headed guy, he had issues and it made it very difficult. The feud was mostly musical, not so much personality. I mean Don was a real belter, singer; he liked, you know the dramatic, and George was a rocker. George liked hard stuff and Don always wanted more lyrical melodic stuff. But I really enjoyed doing the album and I especially enjoyed George's guitar sound and work, he was as good a guitarist as I ever worked with."[93]

With Tom gone, Don once again asked to have Michael Wagener brought aboard. Knowing that Michael didn't do drugs, Don knew that Michael was stable and could help take control.

Recalling the events, Don said, "The album was going south, wasn't going well, it was really a mess. And that's when I went to the record company and threatened, and I said, 'It's over. You're not going to get a record, it's not going to happen. We'd been in the studio for months, we'd spent a quarter of a million dollars, it's all garbage, I need help. Let Michael Wagener come in and help.' I basically said if you don't bring in Michael I quit, it's over, it's done."[94]

Eventually, after much consideration and further threats from Don, Elektra agreed to bring Wagener on. In addition producer Roy Thomas Baker, who was known for having a

---

93 Ibid.
94 Don Dokken interview with James Curl.

white suit and white Rolls-Royce for the day and a black suit and black Rolls-Royce for the night, also came aboard. Roy's job was to more or less help keep the band in check and occupied. To do this, Roy set up blenders to make Pina coladas. He also brought in Pac-Man and pinball machines and used them as diversions to keep the madness down so Michael could concentrate on working.

"And that was Roy Thomas Baker's role. Just keeping the madness down and away from Michael so he could work," said Don. "Roy just came in to keep the peace between George, Jeff, Mick and I, because those guys were out of their minds on coke. All they wanted to do was get out by eleven o'clock so they could get to the Rainbow before last call and chase chicks and do blow. It was an insane time."[95]

Remembering the time, Mick said, "There was a lot of game-playing going on, a lot of drug use and late-night activities."

In addition to the problems with Tom, Geoff and George, the ego clashes and volatility between Don and George was so bad that they refused to work together at the same time in the studio. To lessen the problem, George worked with Jeff and Mick in the afternoon and Don recorded his vocal tracks at night with Michael.

"We had to have schedules," said Don. "George comes in from three to seven and Don will come in and sing from nine to twelve, because we just couldn't be in the studio at the same time, there was just too much tension. George would just make everyone miserable with his complaining and bitching."[96]

While doing his vocal tracks at night Don and Michael would also work on producing the album, which included

---

95 Ibid.
96 Ibid.

working on George's solos in secret. This was done behind George's back. In fact, Don told Michael not to tell George, because if George knew that Don was involved with producing his solos he would refuse to use them. "So basically," said Don, "I would produce from about midnight 'til four in the morning, and Michael is living with me, so we'd go back to the house, and then he'd come in the next day to play it for George, and George would say, 'Cool.' George never knew I was producing his solos."[97]

It was during the making of *Tooth and Nail* that Dokken's publicist decided to play up the feud between Don and George. Speaking of the incident, Pilson said, "It was a drastically over hyped version of something that was essentially true. The two get along pretty good now but there was a time in the early days they didn't get along great. What really blew it all up is when we were doing publicity for the *Tooth and Nail* record. We had a publicist who wanted to come up with a publicity angle that would really help sell the band. So, what they centered on after talking with everybody was 'Wow, Don and George don't like each other,' and that just exploded and it became the media hook that got stuck with the band and then it became a self-fulfilling prophecy and then it became our worst enemy. Did George like the fact that the band was called Dokken? Of course he didn't like that, he just wanted a regular band name."[98]

Despite a mountain of difficulties, *Tooth and Nail* was eventually finished. The album hit the record stores in September of '84 and right from the start it took some time to catch on. The first single "Into the Fire" was released, "And, you know, it didn't go," said Don. Undeterred,

---

97 Ibid.

98 Jeff Pilson states that "feud" between Don Dokken and George Lynch started off as publicity angle, The Metal Voice, by Jimmy Kay, July 5, 2018.

Dokken hit the road to support the album starting in Texas on October 9 with Twisted Sister and Y&T.

Remembering the time Mick said, "Oh God, everything was so cool then. It was so damn exciting. We had better tour buses. We had hidden cameras at the back of the bus and the guys used to make porno tapes with their girls. Oh God, it was drugs and booze and all the chicks were hanging around, and the money started coming in, and big arenas, better drum stuff, bigger, everything was full on ten in motion. It was all just brand new and all going a hundred miles an hour. It was a pretty exciting moment."[99]

Recalling the extracurricular activity that took place at the back of the bus Don remarked, "I keep waiting, literally every six months to a year, I keep waiting for those videos to show up on You Tube. Cause you know we had "the back of the bus productions." And we had two hidden video cameras stuck up where the speakers were supposed to go. And we took the speakers out and put cameras in the back of the bus and we would film what was going on in the back of the bus. And we had hours and hours of girls coming on the bus and that's as far as I'm going to go. And I remember at the end of the tour I thought, 'this shit is gonna come back to haunt me.' And you know Jeff and George and Mick should all say 'thank you, Don, for destroying those tapes,' cause they're all guilty. I could have kept those tapes. I remember once in the back of the bus it was Jeff and me with two beautiful blonds and he was on one couch and I was on the other and we let the good times roll."[100]

Between November of '84 and January of '85 Dokken opened over 40 shows for none other than the legendary Ronnie James Dio. Remembering the time, Jeff remarked,

---

99 Martin Popoff interview with Mick Brown.
100 Don Dokken interview, the Classic Metal Show

"Nearly every night of Dokken's touring with Dio, George Lynch and I would watch the band. They were such a force to be reckoned with."[101]

It was during this time that the band released its second single, "Just Got Lucky," and also filmed a video for the song during a stop in Honolulu, Hawaii. For the video the band decided to get creative. In addition to live concert footage, Dokken's management thought it would be a good idea to film George's guitar solo atop a very live and active volcano. With acrid smoke and steam billowing from a massive crater, George performed his solo during what could only be described as a surreal "Spinal Tap" moment.

"We were up there for so long that seismic activity developed," explained George. "Everyone else had left the park, but we were so off the beaten path, we didn't know. Steam started coming up, it was hard to breathe. Then my shoes broke through lava crust to the hot magma underneath. I could feel the heat and thought to myself, 'Is this normal?' "[102]

As dusk approached and the shoot was ending, park rangers came to warn the group that they had to leave immediately. Shortly after taking off, the volcano blew— hoping to get some extra footage the camera crew spent an hour circling the eruption.

"Just Got Lucky" and its accompanying video helped push the album to 450,000 sales, not quite the 500,000 needed to hit the Gold mark. Dokken wrapped up their tour on April 10, 1985 in Syracuse as the warm up for the red rocker Sammy Hagar. The album however had stalled even

---

101 Jeff Pilson interview with James Curl.
102 Dokken to Lynch Mob to Art, by Michelle Sathe, February 21, 2009.

after a successful tour—that was until the release of the third single, the massive "monster ballad," "Alone Again."

Needing some more momentum to help sell the album, the band did a live concert video for "Alone Again" with footage filmed at the Palladium in L.A. Initially, Elektra didn't want to put the video out, but after repeated threats from Don that he would quit the band, the video was released. And it's a good thing it was. The song would go on to be the band's biggest hit and propel the album from 450,000 to well-over 1,000,000 sales. The LP would eventually peak at a respectable 49 on the *Billboard* 200 album chart and be certified Gold in August of '85.

"Alone Again," would spend 14 weeks on the *Hot Mainstream Rock Tracks* chart, which included two weeks at its peak position of No. 20. Moreover, the melodic ballad was aided by consistent rotation on MTV. This helped give the band their first and biggest hit on the *Billboard Hot 100* chart where it topped out at No. 64 and remained for 11 weeks from May to July 1985.

When asked about the song, Jeff said, "I was very gratified and our managers didn't want it to be released as a single. I have to give Don some credit, he was the one who fought the hardest for it—that it was the right thing to do. I agreed with him absolutely. George and Mick were kind of neutral, but I felt it was a strong song. So, our management agreed to release it as a single and it changed the course of the band."[103]

"Well, I mean, "Alone Again," obviously, was our most famous ballad," explained Don. "And the funny thing was I wrote it when I was 25. And I wrote it on a little four-track recorder, put it on a cassette and it ended up in a box for, like,

---

103 Jeff Pilson interview with James Curl.

eight years. And the record company, on *Tooth and Nail*, our second album, they said ballads are the thing. Journey had a big hit with "Lights" and Night Ranger... Everybody had ballads, and we didn't have any ballads. So I dug out a bunch of tunes, and I went, 'What's this? 'Alone Again,' I don't even remember it.' So I listened to it, and Jeff listened to it, and he said, 'That's a cool chorus. Maybe we can revamp it.' So we recorded "Alone Again." This is a thing I wrote when I was very young, very naïve. Everybody says, 'Who'd you write about?' 'I don't know.' 'What was the girl's name?' 'I don't know.' I must have been in love—it's a very sad song—but I don't remember who I wrote it about. I don't know. It was just a song that came out, I always say, from here (pointing at the sky)—whatever that higher power is."[104]

Although *Tooth and Nail* hadn't stormed out of the gate in terms of fast sales, it did eventually catch on. Helped along by three bonafide hits, the late bloomer eventually received the lofty Platinum certification on March 16, 1989.

Reviews for the album were generally positive from fans and critics alike. The varying tracks offer a wide variety of musical flavors with fast scorchers like "Tooth and Nail" and "Turn on the Action," to the grim and heavy, "When Heaven Comes Down," with its slow, grinding riff and pounding drums.

There are also plenty of catchy rockers like, "Just Got Lucky," "Bullets to Spare," "Don't Close Your Eyes," and "Heartless Heart." And of course the mega-hit, "Alone Again."

---

104 *Blabbermouth*, The story behind Dokken's most famous ballad "Alone Again".

A noticeable difference between *Breaking the Chains* and *T&N* is Don's vocals, which offer up a nice blend of both power and soul. Furthermore, his voice seems to have matured and sounds a little deeper and rough at times. This plays in well to the music style of the songs, especially on the heavier tracks.

Another standout feature of the album is George's blistering guitar work. His soloing cuts like a chainsaw throughout and really shines on tracks like, "Without Warning," "Tooth and Nail" and "Don't Close Your Eyes."

On "Without Warning," the album's opening track, George begins with an intricate acoustic instrumental that slowly builds into distorted and screeching electrical leads. The song displays George's virtuosity and sets the listener up for what's about to come. Speaking of the song, George said, "I think that's something I came up with on my little Fostex X-15 four-track in the wee hours of the morning in my little home situation that I had, for pre-production for *Tooth And Nail*—that's where everything got written. This room we had boarded-up and we just kind of went in there and not take showers and not really come out for very long and just stay in there and grind away and come up with cool stuff; it was really fun."[105]

George's creative guitar work shows why he became one of the most influential and dominant guitarists to come out of the '80s. His playing offers up plenty of ear candy with a potent blend of catchy riffs and aggressive fills that reach out and grab ya. Couple this with Don's powerful singing, Jeff's thumping bass, and Mick's thunderous drumming and you have an album that reaches the upper levels.

---

105 Ye Olde Metal, Dokken's *Tooth and Nail.*

Not every fan, however, felt that *T&N* was great. There were those that thought some of the lyrics were a bit "cheesy" and too full of 80s glam metal fluff. And while these opinions may hold some merit, aside from some lyrical clichés, the album is undoubtedly outstanding. Moreover, *Tooth and Nail* is consistently found lurking in many top 20 or 50 lists of the all-time greatest '80s albums.

With the break-out success of *Tooth and Nail*, Dokken had finally "made it." And though it was the album that pushed Dokken to the next level and brought them out of their starving artist existence, their follow up LP would earn even greater accolades.

Chapter 6
The Flyer Wars
and Hear 'N Aid

Following the breakout success of *T&N* Dokken's popularity exploded and it couldn't have happened at a better time. By late '84 the Strip was entering full hair metal mode. Bands like Mötley Crüe, Ratt, Quiet Riot, Stryper, L.A. Guns, W.A.S.P., and Poison had taken over. Not only did they have an iron grip on the Strip, but MTV and rock stations as well. Dokken now sat alongside the aforementioned bands, and for better or worse, would forever be lumped in with the hair bands of L.A.

It wasn't just the Glam bands that were enjoying a growth spurt, heavy metal was booming as well. Dio had just released *Last in Line,* Judas Priest, *Defenders of the Faith* and Motörhead had come out with *No Remorse.* The albums were selling millions of copies and the bands were gaining international and commercial success at a tremendous pace.

Across the pond in Europe several of the "New Wave of British Heavy Metal" bands were also becoming increasingly popular. Def Leppard and Iron Maiden in particular had broken into the American market and were rapidly becoming household names. And the momentous rise of heavy metal didn't end there. Other bands like Whitesnake, Guns N' Roses and Bon Jovi were on the prowl and about to become rock 'n' roll Gods.

While hard rock and heavy metal was shifting into high gear, thrash and speed metal was also being developed and sharpened to a razor fine edge. Bands like Metallica, Slayer,

Anthrax, and Megadeth had taken influences from the likes of Diamond Head, Motörhead, Venom and Angel Witch and stepped on the throttle. The result was two indelible black marks down the highway to hell.

As hard rock and heavy metal began entering its prime years, globally the response was phenomenal. In America, fans couldn't get enough and it was a great time to be alive. Our favorite bands were writing the soundtrack that would define an entire generation, and everyone seemed to be young. As the music grew so did the concerts; and they weren't just concerts, they were events. Massive arenas packed with 25,000 or more crazed fans complete with visually stunning stage shows and big productions.

At the time, before the advent of the Internet, people stood in line for hours to get a ticket to these shows days or even weeks in advance. With a ticket in hand they waited excitedly for the day to arrive. When it finally came, concert-goers would spend hours getting ready, especially the girls. With a can of Aqua Net hair spray and a brush they teased their hair to gigantic proportions and made sure their fishnet stockings and denim miniskirts were just right and tight. From there everyone would typically pile into a cool old Camaro or Mustang and head to the show; all the while blasting from a tape deck the bands they were about to see.

With the youth of America going crazy for rock 'n' roll the popularity of L.A's music scene continued to grow. This in turn caused a huge influx of musicians and bands that arrived on the Strip with dreams of rock 'n' roll stardom. Unfortunately, most had only seen the glamorous portrait painted in MTV videos or magazines; the brutal reality was much worse and shocking. The Strip was a "musical war zone" and the competition was ferocious. Most of the bands that showed up hadn't taken this into consideration. The truth was, there were about a thousand bands that were far more talented, better looking and more street wise. Moreover, drug addiction was rampant and the town was swarming with record executives looking to take advantage of a naive band—most didn't have a chance.

If a young band was lucky maybe they grabbed a moment of fleeting fame. Maybe one day they could tell their kids about how they once opened for Great White or L.A. Guns at the Whisky a Go Go—or how they partied with the guys from Mötley Crüe and Ratt at the Rainbow. Most however had no chance of success and were ground up by the cogs of the music scene and tossed aside—their dreams crushed by cruel reality. Realizing that they weren't gonna "make it" they went running back to whatever town they dared to venture out of; hopefully without an addiction to a drug or a nasty STD.

Nevertheless, the hopefuls swarmed in and at any given time there were hundreds of bands living on or near the Strip—many of them in vans or cars. These bands were in constant, and at time physical, competition to increase their fan base and get people to the shows. The problem was, with so many bands vying for a shot at rock stardom, how do you get your name out there? This was before the Internet and cell phones, so there were no websites, Facebook or Twitter to advertise upcoming shows. If a band was lucky, and could afford it, they could hire a manager or advertise in one of the local publications like *Bam Magazine,* but most were too strapped to do it.

It was around this time that the now famous "Flyer Wars" began. Bands would print up stacks of flyers and staple them to wooden telephone poles, or tape them to electrical utility boxes and any available wall. Though technically illegal, it was free advertising. Another method was to walk up and down the Strip handing out flyers and talking with people to try and generate interest.

Bands had been plastering the Strip with flyers for years, however not to the extent that the mid '80s experienced. At its peak, the city of West Hollywood had to hire a crew to come in with brooms and a truck to clean up the mountainous piles of discarded flyers that littered the sidewalks and filled the gutters.

At first the flyers worked well and the bands were courteous towards one another—this however did not last long. That's when the real "Flyer Wars" started. As fast as a band could staple a flyer another band would come by, tear it down and put up their own. Another strategy was to take as many flyers from the person handing them out and toss them into the nearest trash can.

"Are you kidding me, man?" said Jack Russell, who was a frequent participant in the Flyer Wars. "One day I remember we had a truck and I'm up there pounding our flyer into a telephone pole and I look behind me about a block away and there's Nikki Sixx pounding his flyers over ours. So we turn around the next block and we come up behind him and we put ours over his. And we would go up the street and pound more over his. And pretty soon we'd see him come back to the start. It was like who's gonna run out of flyers first or nails, ya know. But it was fun, we all had a laugh about it. You know, I mean really as much rivalry as there was we were all friends. I mean we all hung out and partied together."[106]

When asked if he ever participated in the "Flyer Wars," Don replied, "Oh God, don't I know it. Not in Dokken, but in Airborn I did. Me and my original bass player Jeff Tappan and Bobby Blotzer would go to the print shop and make those flyers and just walk up and down Sunset. And you know you put your flyer up and somebody covers it up and on the way back you tear theirs off and put yours back up.[107]

"But we had a great trick which really helped Airborn in the early days and that was the Starwood. And the Starwood had a policy that you could have an open guest list, be it ten people or a thousand people. So, we would go down on the beach, 'hey, man, I'm Don, I'm in this band called Airborn, you should come to the show, I'll put you on the guest list.' We would just walk up and down the strand cause I lived down by the beach. And we would turn in our guest list typed up very nicely, not handwritten, alphabetically. And this is a place that only holds 700 people and we turn in our guest list with 500 people. And we figured if only 20 to 25 percent showed up we were golden."[108]

As the "Flyer Wars" raged on the Strip, big things were happening in music. It was during this time that it became in vogue for artists to participate in charity events aimed at famine relief for Africa.

In 1984 a mega-group known as Band Aid was formed to raise money to feed the starving in Ethiopia. The group consisted of nearly 40 musicians from mostly the alternative

---

106 Jack Russell interview with James Curl.
107 Don Dokken interview with James Curl.
108 Ibid.

genre. The list was quite impressive, featuring Bono from U2, Phil Collins of Genesis, George Michael and Sting, as well as Boy George and members of Duran Duran. Together the assembled musicians recorded the song, "Do They Know It's Christmas?" The single was released on December 3, 1984 and went on to become a massive hit selling millions of copies and topping charts all over the world.

Next up came the charity song, "We Are The World," written by Michael Jackson and Lionel Richie in March of 1985. Like its predecessor, it featured an impressive star-studded lineup consisting of a plethora of top performers like, Tina Turner, Stevie Wonder, Billy Joel, Bob Dylan, Bruce Springsteen and Diana Ross along with many more. It too became a huge commercial success and raised millions of dollars to feed the hungry. It also became the fastest selling pop single in history and was the first single to be certified Quadruple Platinum.

With everyone seemingly getting involved in a charity event, it was rock 'n' roll's turn to muscle in and do its part.

In 1985 Vivian Campbell and Jimmy Bain (of the band Dio) attended a 48-hour radiothon called "Rock Relief for Africa" put on by the L.A. station 95.5 KLOS. During the event, Vivian and Jimmy realized that participation from the heavy metal community was practically non-existent. It didn't take long however for the imaginative pair to come up with an idea to write a song geared around the heavy metal genre. The song would generate money and awareness for famine relief in Africa.

"We're doing the interview," said Campbell, "and it was at the time that 'We Are the World,' that Michael Jackson project had come out. The DJ said to us 'how come no one, absolutely no one, in the rock community was invited to participate in this?' and you know when you think about it, back in that era hard rock music sold millions of records but it didn't have any sort of respect in the music industry. It never won Grammys or anything, it was always kind of frowned upon. So, we kind of had a bit of conversation on air with the DJ about that and we kind of jokingly said that we should do our own thing, and Jimmy came up with the name right there and then and said, 'we should call it Hear 'n Aid.' We all kind of fell off our stools laughing about that and at the time Jimmy and I lived together; we were roommates during those early Dio records. We went back to our apartment later that night and you know, we said hey, let's give it some serious consideration. Let's actually look into the possibilities of doing this. We wrote the song that night."[109]

Jimmy and Vivian knew that the idea was an incredibly ambitious venture. They also knew that they couldn't accomplish the project without a strong leader, so they approached Ronnie with the idea. Initially, Ronnie was cold toward the proposal and showed little interested in getting involved. "He wasn't on-board with it at first," said Campbell. "He wasn't against the idea, but we just had so much going on, like I said he was producing the record, he was writing all the lyrics for Sacred Heart. I think he felt overwhelmed."[110] Eventually, after weeks of pestering by Viv and Jimmy, Ronnie agreed to discuss the idea with Wendy. Finally, after some deliberation, they agreed to get involved and came up with a plan.

---

109 *Shutupandrockon.com,* interview with Vivian Campbell, March 4, 2017.
110 *Shutupandrockon.com,* interview with Vivian Campbell, March 4, 2017.

The first, and perhaps the biggest challenge, was to get in touch with as many big-name rockers as possible and get them to agree to help. With a course of action laid out, Vivian and Jimmy along with Wendy began the arduous task of reaching out to some of Metal's most notable "stars." This took weeks of tedious phone calls to managers and agents but eventually yielded great results; 40 of rock's biggest A-listers answered the call and agreed to contribute.

"I spent literally weeks and weeks making phone calls to people," said Vivian, "just 'hi, you don't know me but I'm Vivian Campbell, I play guitar for Dio,' and gave them the whole spiel about this is what we're doing and is there any way you can participate. We pulled it off, it was incredibly hard work. But you know, I don't think we would have been able to do it without Ronnie lending his support."[111]

Dokken was one of the bands that Vivian reached out to and the guys readily agreed to participate. Because of his unique and outstanding vocals, Don was offered a spot as one of the lead vocalists. He would share the spotlight with an impressive gathering of heavyweight singers that included, Ronnie Dio, Dave Meniketti, Eric Bloom, Kevin DuBrow, Rob Halford, Paul Shortino, and Geoff Tate. Each singer was designated with a specific part to sing.

To complement the vocals an equally impressive group of guitar shredders and virtuosos was brought together. Because of his skills, George was selected as one of the lead guitarists to participate in the song's monstrously epic three minute solo.

"I was pretty nervous," said George. It was right at the height of the '80s guitar mania, and here is every freaking

---

111 *Shutupandrockon.com*, interview with Vivian Campbell, March 4, 2017.

guitar player. We were outside Charlie Chaplin's old movie lot in Los Angeles. Everyone was there—Yngwie, Neal Schon. And I was like, 'oh my god.' I was totally unprepared. We're all sitting outside, and you get your 30 minutes or an hour. It was a lot of pressure. But I gotta say if you listen to the audio recording of it, you can really differentiate one guitar player from the next. But if you watch the video it's really cool. Everyone's taking different takes. It was a great experience. Ronnie was a gentleman and a gracious human being."[112]

Like Don, George would share the spotlight with a renowned group of lightning fingered virtuosos, with each getting a moment to display their superlative skills. The impressive gathering of axemen was without a doubt one of the finest ever assembled for any project, and was comprised of, Vivian Campbell, Carlos Cavazo, Buck Dharma, Brad Gillis, Craig Goldy, Yngwie Malmsteen, Eddie Ojeda, and Neal Schon. Iron Maiden's Dave Murray and Adrian Smith were in the middle of their "World Slavery Tour" at the time, but were able to fly in and attend the main recording session as rhythm guitarists.

In addition to the fine group of singers and guitar players an equally prestigious group of rock stars was assembled to sing background vocals in a choir-like setting. This group consisted of Tommy Aldridge, Dave Alford, Carmine Appice, Vinny Appice, Jimmy Bain, Frankie Banali, Mick Brown, Vivian Campbell, Carlos Cavazo, Amir Derakh, Buck Dharma, Brad Gillis, Craig Goldy, Chris Hagar, Chris Holmes, Blackie Lawless, George Lynch, Yngwie

---

112 *Blabbermouth,* George Lynch: Bodybuilding was one of the silliest thing I've ever done.

Malmsteen, Mick Mars, Michael McKean, Vince Neil, Ted Nugent, Eddie Ojeda, Jeff Pilson, Rudy Sarzo, Claude Schnell, Neal Schon, Harry Shearer, Mark Stein and Matt Thorr.

Bass duties were handled by Jimmy Bain, keyboards by Claude Schnell and drums were covered by Vinny Appice and Frankie Banali, respectively.

On May 20 long limousines and luxury sedans began dropping off rock stars at A&M Records Studios in Hollywood for the two-day recording session. To add a little comedy relief, Michael McKean and Harry Shearer, better known as David St. Hubbins and Derek Smalls of the parody band Spinal Tap, were also in attendance and in character. Not only did they have everyone laughing, they were also there to lend their "mighty pipes" to the choir as well. "I've got pipes," said Davis St. Hubbins. "I've got pipes I haven't used yet."

"I wore a white suit," said Don. "I did it on purpose because I knew everybody was going to show up in leather jackets. I wanted to stand out. God bless Ronnie. He kept making fun of my suit and telling me that GQ was calling. I said I wanted to look different."[113]

Recalling the unique gathering, Vivian said, "You put a bunch of eighties guitarists in the same room and, of course, there's going to be competition for bragging rights. They were even arguing about who had the biggest hair."

Remembering the day, Jeff said, "The only day I was involved was the day we did all the background vocals. It was actually a really really fun day. I was actually very proud of both Don and George because both their contributions on

---

113 Don Dokken interview with James Curl.

the song were very unique, and I thought both of them did an amazing job. We were still on the up and up and we were still a force, yes, there was always the contention in the band but for the most part we were pretty strong, so it was really fun. The background vocal day was a whole day doing background vocals at A&M studios, lots of friends there. And it ended up at a huge party at Kevin DuBrow's house, it was crazy and everything you could imagine. I do remember, my very last memory, we somehow ended up at Mick Brown's hotel room with Eddie Ojeda from Twisted Sister singing Beatles songs at seven in the morning. It was just bizarre. I don't even remember how we got there."[114]

With the group assembled and cameras rolling, recording began for the song "Stars" and ran through the following day. From there it was then added to a compilation album that contained live tracks by, Kiss, Motörhead, Dio, Accept, Rush and Scorpions, as well as studio recordings by Y&T and Jimi Hendrix.

Originally the *Hear 'n Aid* album, along with a documentary that had captured the whole event, was slated to be released shortly after recording. However, because of contractual problems with some of the artist's record labels the release date was pushed back to January 1, 1986. The six month delay somewhat reduced the impact of the album, but nonetheless it went on to raise over $1,000,000 within the first year and over $3,000,000 since then. All in all the effort was seen as a success and the song "Stars" was a hit. It also showed that even the so-called "bad boys" of rock 'n' roll had heart and could care.

---

114 Jeff Pilson interview with James Curl.

Chapter 7
Under Lock and Key

The Hear 'n Aid project had been a lot of fun for the guys, but it was now time for Dokken to get back to some serious work; which meant writing the follow-up to *Tooth and Nail*.

With the success of *T&N* the guys knew they had to write an album that would stand up to its predecessor, which would be no easy task. The Dokken machine, however was primed and at this point the guys were entering the peak of their musical powers.

Work began on the record in late spring of '85 and ran through the summer. Unlike *Tooth and Nail* the writing process for *Under Lock and Key* was a lot smoother.

"Under Lock and Key I would say of all the Dokken albums was our most collaborative record," explained Don. "We actually got a rehearsal room and said 'what do you got? What do you got? What do you got?' And George would come up with a riff and Jeff had a song and I had a song, it was very collaborative. The classic example is "The Hunter." George showed up with a riff and he said this is gonna be my instrumental on the album. And I said you gotta be kidding me, it's too slow, medium tempo, it's boring, you wanna shred over this? So he said, 'fuck you, this is gonna be my instrumental and that's it.' So I said let me just take the song home at least and take a crack at it. And I took it home to my apartment and I wrote "The Hunter."[115]

"I wouldn't say more cohesive as much as more collaborative," explained Jeff. *"Tooth and Nail* was very

------

115 Don Dokken interview with James Curl.

cohesive with George and I, and then Don added some real strong contributions, but *ULnK* was more collaborative all around. It was our peak of efficiency and everyone really being on their game. I remember starting a lot of the music on the road in hotel rooms with George. Then we had a couple weeks of Don and I (and sometimes Mick) working in Don's apartment (nicknamed the Hobbit house cuz of what it looked like—it was an old movie star apartment complex from the '40s). Very inspired work. Then the final pre-production saw some real tying up of loose ends. It was great and we really were quite focused as a group. Good times!"[116]

By September the LP was completed and the guys were ready to get back on the road. To start off a new tour cycle Dokken headed over to Japan for their inaugural visit to the "land of the rising sun," but certainly not their last.

They arrived in late November and played five shows, two in Tokyo, one in Osaka, one in Nagoya and a final show back in Tokyo. Due to the success of *Tooth and Nail* and the overwhelming popularity of rock 'n' roll, Dokken was already well-know and received a tremendous welcome from eager fans wanting to see them.

Recalling the first tour Jeff said, "The reception was amazing. The funniest thing I remember is that you know the bootlegger used to obviously communicate by telephone back then and the record had not come out in Japan, we went in November of '85 and *Under Lock and Key* did not come out there right away, so we brought some with us. But when we got there we saw a bunch of bootleg t-shirts that had been made that said, 'Under the Rock and Key.' So obviously someone on the phone said, (in their Japanese accent), "'the

---

116 Jeff Pilson interview with James Curl.

record called, 'Under the Rock and Key.' "[117] It was indeed a hilarious "Spinal Tap" moment that Jeff now remembers with a hearty laugh.

Jeff then went on to say, "The reception was amazing, the people there were great. The shows went great, I mean it really snapped us into a really good space. That was probably one of the best times we ever had as a group. Certainly all the times we went to Japan, but that first time was really, really special. Really made a big impression and the shows were amazing."[118]

Being in such an exotic country there were numerous tourist attractions to see, however the guys were hardly thinking of such things. When asked if they spent any time seeing the sights Jeff replied, "Well we went to Nagoya Castle and took some photos there, but not a whole lot. I mean we were into the old partying and hanging out with the girls and all of that; and there was a lot of that more than anything. We were kids in a candy store basically."[119]

"Well it was just a shock," said Don. "I had never been to Japan. Anybody who has ever been there knows it's not like going to Europe, Italy, Germany or France. It's a very different culture. We got off the plane and there were hundreds of Japanese girls with presents. They were throwing the presents over the wall at us as we came through customs. That was kind of shocking, we kind of felt like we were the Beatles. We didn't expect it and nobody warned me.

"We couldn't leave the hotels," said Don. "There were people camping outside the hotels. They had candlelight

---

117 Jeff Pilson interview with James Curl.
118 Ibid.
119 Ibid.

vigils. I used to get up in the morning and look out the window and people would wave and cry and scream and holler. It was pretty intense. When you're young it was obviously an ego boost."[120]

Continuing on Don said, "The shows were off the hook and sold out everywhere. A couple of the shows we took a train to and we had to time it. Like the train leaves at 4:05 so at 4:03 it would pull up and the doors would open and we would have to run to the train and have police with barricades holding people back so they wouldn't get to us. It was pretty intense."[121]

Back in the States, *Under Lock and Key* was making the executives at Elektra very happy. Having been released on November 22, fan reaction to the album was overwhelmingly positive. At record stores across America copies were being bought up as fast as the shelves were stocked. On March 4, 1986, less than three months after its release, the record went gold. Just over 12 months later, on April 14, 1987 it would reach the much coveted platinum mark.

Moreover, the album hurled Dokken into the Top Forty for the first time reaching number 32 on the U.S. *Billboard* 200 where it remained for 67 weeks. The record also produced two hit singles, "The Hunter," and "In My Dreams," with each reaching 25 and 24 respectively on *Billboard*'s Mainstream Rock and getting their fair share of MTV time.

If *T&N* was the album that brought Dokken to everyone's attention, *ULnK* made them rock stars. The record would go on to be regarded by most as Dokken's greatest opus. The

---

120 Don Dokken interview with James Curl.
121 Ibid.

band followed the same formula as *T&N* by giving the fans an album that was diverse; yet at the same time reaching further in every musical direction.

Don's powerful vocals are smooth, intense, and full of soul. George's guitar work and tone, arguably stands unmatched on anything he has ever done, prior or since. Like some thunder god Mick pounds the drums with concussive force, especially noticeable on the song "Lightning Strikes Again," while Jeff's bass playing is tight and precise.

Speaking of the album, Jeff gave his feelings saying, "I will say it's not my favorite, but in some ways it's the best. It was certainly the pinnacle of our working relationship, we were still very much a band at that point."[122]

Jeff went on to explain, "The collaboration with Dokken was always quirky but I think that was the peak of its effectiveness. There were still two separate writing camps. It was either me and George, sometimes with Mick, or me and Don, sometime with Mick, never all four of us and it stayed that way throughout the entire '80s. It was an odd working relationship.

"Under Lock and Key we were at our peak, we were still pretty damn hungry because you know *Tooth and Nail* did well and it definitely took us a notch farther but in our minds it still didn't take us as far as Mötley Crüe and Ratt were. So we were very hungry, we were very motivated and very focused. Everybody was kind of at their peak in terms of writing and I think it was our most fluid writing era and the most cohesive.

"The problem with that record for me is that when I hear it now it is so time stamp dated. *Tooth and Nail* is a dryer,

---

122 Jeff Pilson interview with James Curl.

more raw record, so I think it stood the test of time better. *Under Lock and Key* has some great songs, some of my favorite songs are on that record. I love "It's Not Love," it's one of my favorite Dokken songs. But even that is more slick than I would have liked. "In My Dreams" is too slick, it was just a little too slick. Too many effects, too many of the '80s time stamp on there that I wish could be redone, but obviously it is what it is."[123]

Don also felt that the album was the best he and his bandmates had done saying, "I think so. In the Dokken days that was probably our pinnacle. It was an album that we all actually pulled together and wrote together for a change."[124]

Though the record was a big hit, some found it to be a bit ostentatious and the more polished production less to their taste. The slower love songs like, "Slipping Away" and "Jaded Heart" were too effusive and dripping with gushy emotions for fans of the heavier *Tooth and Nail*; but then again, you can't satisfy everyone.

As hair metal was now in its prime years, Dokken opted to try and fit in. The album cover featured the boys in colorful outfits and teased out "Big Hair." Although the album strived for a bit more of the "Glam" look in terms of image, the music was unmistakably Dokken. There are some great head-banging rockers, like the speed-metal, "Till the Living End" and "Lightning Strikes Again." Mid-temp melodic tracks like, "Unchain the Night" and "The Hunter" and of course a couple of syrupy ballads to satisfy one's sweet tooth—or broken heart. In addition, several of the songs

---

123 Ibid.
124 Don Dokken interview with James Curl.

really stand out with some evocative vocal harmonies that show just how talented Jeff and Mick are as singers.

Overall, the album represent the pinnacle of Dokken's discography and metallic might and is the one by which all others are judged.

Critical reviews were somewhat varied. Music writer Eduardo Rivadavia in his review for AllMusic calls *Under Lock and Key,* "quite possibly Dokken's most 'complete' album, with a little something for every type of fan," like "fist-pumping headbangers," extraordinary "bittersweet mid-paced rockers and 'saccharine ballads.' " Rivadavia recommends the album as the best introduction to new listeners of Dokken, but notes that heavy metal purists would likely prefer the band's 1984 album *Tooth and Nail.*"[125]

Martin Popoff the famed music journalist and writer of all things heavy metal considers the album "too weighted towards Def Leppard's fat-and-open formula rock," and as a result "a bit subdued and predictable" in comparison with its predecessor. The band's glamorous look, the media exposure and George Lynch's "attempt to define the L.A. sound in his own image" do not save *Under Lock and Key* from sounding "like the work of a band just fed."[126]

Having conquered Japan, Dokken was back in L.A. by early December. Following a month off, the guys spent March and April of '86 in Europe playing gigs with Accept.

"That was a very important tour for us," remarked Jeff. "A lot of learning on that tour. Accept were such a tight, pro band and we admired them greatly. They really knew how to groove in a very heavy way that we loved. Plus they were

---

125 Wikipedia, Under Lock and Key.
126 Ibid.

dedicated and hard working. It was no fluke that they were that great. We also had a lot of fun with them but I know they looked at us as sometimes being "off the rails."

"I remember one incident where we had a long bus ride one night from France into Belgium. Mick ended up getting off the bus at the border to use the bathroom and he forgot to do the tradition of leaving the bay key in the driver's seat to let him know someone is off the bus.

"Anyways, it was a rare instance of the Belgians basically just waving us through, so Mick got left behind. We didn't discover it till we got to the hotel in Belgium. And because he had no ID, no clue where we were going, and this was 1986 so certainly no cellphones that became a problem. Anyways, after hours of grilling by the Belgians, they finally made some calls and found where Mick was supposed to be going and he ended up with a $200 cab ride to where he needed to be. We all thought that was hilarious—the guys from Accept did NOT find that funny. They were horrified. They were pretty damn serious, we must have looked so young and reckless to them.

"Well I'm a lot older now, and honestly it's still extremely hilarious to me!!!!!!"[127]

Unfortunately for Dokken the Accept tour had to be cut short because of the Chernobyl nuclear disaster that took place on April 25 in northern Ukraine. Due to the nuclear reactor's explosion, and resulting fire, massive plumes of smoke carrying lethal doses of radiation were spewed into the atmosphere. Because the radioactive cloud was reported to be over parts of Sweden, where Dokken was supposed to

---

127 Jeff Pilson interview with James Curl.

play, the guys decided not to take any chances and headed back to America.

Back in the States, the guys got to work quickly on a new video for the song "It's Not Love." With MTV becoming a cultural phenomenon by the mid-1980s, music videos were all the rage. Because of this, bands were able to get massive amounts of exposure. The competition, however, was fierce and artists were constantly forced to come up with new and exciting videos.

For the video the guys teamed up with Wayne Isham, an award-winning video director that had worked with the likes of Bon Jovi, Judas Priest, and Michael Jackson. With Wayne at the reins they came up with an idea that had never been attempted before and was somewhat ground-breaking.

The video featured a buxom blonde in a cowboy hat and tight 501s driving a black Kenworth diesel around L.A. Perched atop the flatbed trailer was Dokken, complete with a working PA system that was cranked to 11 and blaring out, "It's Not Love." In tow was a camera crew filming it all. As one might imagine, having a popular band on a flatbed cruising the Sunset Strip drew a lot of attention.

Remembering the filming of the video Don said, "We got four tickets. We started out in North Hollywood and we got a ticket for noise and we got a ticket in West Hollywood for noise. We ended up at the Rainbow and we got a ticket for that. They started talking about it on the radio saying, 'Dokken is going down Sunset and Hollywood Boulevard!' and people just started following us down the street.

"It looks easy on the video," remarked Don. "But when you're going down the street on a semi-truck bumping around you're hanging on for dear life thinking you're gonna fall off and get ran over. If you look at the video you'll notice I am hanging onto Mick's drum cage a lot because I'm gonna fall of this fucking thing. But it was a fun video."[128]

Recalling his experience with the video Jeff said, "By then we had a little bit of clout and by then we had also met Wayne Isham and he had a place called the Company and they were great people. We got along great and they really really put a lot of work into our videos, so the videos became much more positive by that point.

"We had a PA on the truck that was crankin' the song so we could mime to it. And it was loud and we were trying to cause a scene and the whole thing that happened at the Rainbow at the end was all organic. We pulled up and this crowd just developed and they went along with us and to this day we still say we were the only band that played the Rainbow. And the cops eventually shut us down.

"It was just a wild video and you know the funny thing is we had just gotten back from Europe and in fact it was a European tour we cut short because Chernobyl went off. When Chernobyl went we were headed to Sweden and we were hearing that the nuclear cloud and everything was flying right over Sweden. And so we were freaked out by that and I think we canceled six shows. But before we left Europe, I ended up getting a really bad stomach parasite. So when we were doing the video I was still recovering from that and we had to get a portable driving toilet to follow us everywhere. And between every take I had to go run off into this little porta potty thing that was following us around, it was kinda

---

128 Don Dokken interview with James Curl.

miserable that day. But hey, it doesn't show on the video. It all came out good, let's put it that way."[129]

With videos on consistent rotation on MTV and two hit albums, Dokken's popularity had risen rapidly within the last three years. As their fame grew and began to peak in 1987 the need for anonymity became increasingly necessary.

"When we went on tour," said Don, "when we got really famous we couldn't check into the hotels under our own names, so Jeff was Rufus Green Jeans, (after a character from the television show Captain Kangaroo). Mick was Sam Samsonite, like the suitcase, and I was Dr. G Imsick, and George came up with Mr. Scary. Those were our quote unquote fake names.

"We were actually somewhere in Connecticut or something and the guy at the desk called the cops on us and said there are these guys staying here and these names don't make sense, and I think these guys are drug dealers. And the cops showed up and banged on all our doors and made us come out of the hotel rooms, lean up against the walls, spread our legs, the whole enchilada and show ID's.

"Our road manager said, 'dude, it's Dokken, they can't check in under their real names because there's always fans out there.' So that was an interesting experience."[130]

On May 4, 1986 Dokken hit the road with Judas Priest, who was on their Fuel for Life tour to support their *Turbo* album. The first stop was at the Denver Coliseum. From there they would play a dozen shows across America with the heavy metal legends.

---

129 Jeff Pilson interview with James Curl.
130 Don Dokken interview with James Curl.

Talking of the tour with Priest, Jeff said, "It was great. They were really at the top of their game at that point, they were great every night and they were very cool to us. We were on a pretty high trajectory ourselves so it was a good spot for us. We had a lot of great shows and we had full crowds by the time we got in there. It was just very very positive."[131]

"The *Turbo* tour was a great tour because you know it was a very heavy album," said Don. "It was a heavier audience I'd say, a little more dude oriented and they were at their pinnacle, so between the two of us having multi-platinum albums it was intense, it was sold out every night 15,000 people."[132]

It was on the Priest tour that Don really felt that Dokken had finally "made it."

"We respected Judas Priest," said Don, "they were icons, they were rock gods, but we were holding our own every night and we were getting just as much applause as they were and I thought, 'well, we've arrived.' "[133]

Having spent a couple of months on the road with Priest, the Dokken machine was hitting on all cylinders and ready for more. In August the guys branched off and did a show with Loverboy. Then in October they teamed up with Aerosmith who was on their Permanent Vacation tour. The tour was Aerosmith's first since completing drug rehab and becoming clean and sober.

"We were terrorizing still," said Don. "We were kind of in our terrorizing mode. Aerosmith—that was their first

---

131 Jeff Pilson interview with Jams Curl.
132 Don Dokken interview with James Curl.
133 Ibid.

sober tour. We weren't really allowed to hang with them 'case we'd corrupt them." Don then said jokingly, "You don't want to hang with 'Wild' Mick Brown as you get in all sorts of trouble.

"I remember one night," said Don, "Aerosmith was having a little party back stage, (to celebrate their Permanent Vacation album going Gold), it was their first sober tour I call it, they had all been drug addicts for years and they said keep Dokken away from Aerosmith. And I'm sucking on my wine and valium and the other guys are doing blow."[134]

"With Aerosmith," explained Jeff, "they were just so cool to us. It was the peak of our success, and a period when we were drawing a lot. We would have a full crowd when we would go on at the beginning of the night. It almost felt like we were a co-headliner. Aerosmith was great to us. They were really supportive, the camaraderie with everybody was great. They were real pros and they are not uptight. So many bands tended to be really uptight. They would try to do things to your sound and not let you have lights. Aerosmith was the opposite. They said, 'You guys do whatever you want. We want your show to be great.' They weren't threatened by us. It was really a pleasant, eye-opening experience because their professionalism and positiveness was really powerful."[135]

"I think the Aerosmith tour we were at our best," remarked George, "as far as being at the top of our game as a band. I think we gave them a run for their money a lot of nights, if not better than that. I think we did pretty good and

---

134 Ibid.
135 Jeff Pilson interview with James Curl.

a lot of people were there to see us and we got paid pretty well."[136]

"We were spot on, we'd come into our own so to speak," said Don. "After a couple of world tours we had gotten it figured out, we knew what to do with an arena audience, we knew how to behave and pace ourselves when you're playing four shows a week and sitting on a bus eight to ten hours a night. The Aerosmith tour was amazing."[137]

Recalling a funny incident that happened on their last night with Aerosmith, Don said, "Well one of the funniest things we ever did was our last night with Aerosmith. Aerosmith had that song "Angel," and we took George, which isn't something he would usually do because he is such a serious guy, and we put wings on him. We bought some wings at a prop shop and we gave him a pillow with feathers and we hoisted him up with a harness. And when they sang "Angel," we hoisted him up and he was flying back and forth over the stage and throwing feathers down on the stage. And the guys in Aerosmith just totally cracked up. They thought it was funny.

"So George is just flying around, but the funny thing was is A that George did it, which we were all shocked about, but then B we left him there. We figured we would just tie him off and leave him there for a while. So he was like, 'Ok, we're done, you can let me down' and then we just left him up there which was kind of funny.

"And the last song they did was "Dude Looks Like a Lady," we put Mick in a full-blown red sequin dress, in drag. Our makeup girl put him in drag, full-on makeup, high heels, the stockings, the whole nine yards. I mean he looked like a

---

136 You Tube interview George Lynch.
137 Don Dokken interview with James Curl.

chick, boobs, bra, and I swear, for about five seconds when he walked out Steven Tyler thought he was a chick. And he went up and started grabbing and hugging Steven, and then I think Steven started to realize that that was one ugly chick."[138]

Despite having a hit album and being on a great tour there were cracks in the Dokken foundation that were beginning to spread. Don was slowly becoming isolated within his own band. "Mick and George and Jeff had a bond," he said, "and that was drugs. The three of them would get an ounce of coke and go off and do their thing. I've never done cocaine in my life."[139]

Unhappy with the situation, Don threatened to quit in the midst of the Aerosmith tour. "Too much coke, they were too coked out," said Don. "They were doing massive amounts of cocaine, Jeff and Mick and George, massive booze, massive drugs. And I said, 'we're gonna crash and burn and you guys gotta pull it together or we're gonna fail.' You know I wasn't pointing the finger because I didn't do coke, they were just way over the top, I mean we're talkin' ounces and ounces a week. It was a great tour and a bad tour. Several times George passed out on stage in front of 10,000 people, just passed out cause he was coked up and hadn't slept in two days. And I just said, 'I'm gonna quit. If you don't stop I can't continue, I'm not going down with the ship."[140]

"The first announcement came on Halloween night in Providence, Rhode Island of '87," said Jeff. "He announced

---

138 Popoff Archive, 3: Hair Metal, Don Dokken, By Martin Popoff, Power Chord Press 2017.
139 Dokken: The Hair Metal Band that Hated Itself, by Paul Elliot, October 2, 2015.
140 Don Dokken interview with James Curl.

to us that he planned on leaving unless things really really changed. And what was funny about that is this was during the Aerosmith tour, and during the tour that was the best we he had gotten along. The weeks leading up to that decision were ironically the best we had ever gotten along.

"I remember many nights being in the front of the bus with Don and George and our road manager, later on our manager, Rick Sales, drinking wine and having really nice talks about life. I mean it was absolutely the best we had ever gotten along, so it was an odd time for him to make that announcement. And I think he was sincere and he really did plan on leaving unless things changed, but at the same time it really did kill the morale. And then things started to go downhill fast."[141]

---

141 Jeff Pilson interview with James Curl.

The first incarnation of Dokken, Steven R. Barry, Greg
Pecka and a smiling Don Dokken, circa 1979,
courtesy of Steven R. Barry

Left to right, Steven R. Barry, Don Dokken,
Greg Pecka, circa 1979

The Boyz, May 1976, from left to right Monte Zufelt, George Lynch, Mick Brown, Michael White

Michael, George, Mick, Monte, May 1976

George, Michael, Monte, Mick, May 1976

Monte, George, Mick, Michael, May 1976

Monte, Mick, George and Michael, May 1976

Monte, George, Michael and Mick, May 1976

Courtesy of David Wilson

Courtesy of David Wilson

Courtesy of David Wilson

Courtesy of David Wilson

Unknown, Jack Russell, unknown, John Strednansky,
Don Dokken, Michael Wagener, 1983

Early shot of Don

Dokken circa 1984

The guys, April of 1988

Don, November of 1987
photo by David Plastik

Don, July of 1988
photo by David Plastik

George, 1986
photo by David Plastik

George, 1988 Monsters of Rock tour
photo by David Plastik

A glammed up Jeff Pilson 1986
photo by David Plastik

Jeff, Monsters of Rock tour 1988
photo by Mark Weiss

Mick, Monsters of Rock tour 1988
photo by Mark Weiss

Chapter 8
Back for the Attack
and Freddy Krueger

Although Don's threat of leaving the band brought morale to an all-time low, Dokken's rise in popularity and album sales seemed to be unstoppable.

It was during their tour with Aerosmith that Dokken released their fourth studio album *Back for the Attack* on November 2, 1987. Despite many problems while writing and recording the album, the record was another huge success and proved to be a fast seller going platinum in just three weeks. In addition, it would also become Dokken's all-time bestselling album to date.

Shortly after its release, the record reached No. 13 on the U.S. *Billboard* 200 where it remained for 33 weeks. Three hit singles also charted on *Billboard*'s Mainstream Rock chart. "Dream Warriors" reached No. 22, "Prisoner" No. 37, and "Burning Like a Flame" peaked at No. 20.

Music journalist Martin Popoff praised the album, which "offers length, variation and a sense of ambition as never before," and called it "one of those lost records brimming with bravado" but not so unique to be "one's life soundtrack." He added that the "excruciating" circumstances of its recording took their toll as the band tried to assemble "a more competent, mature, substantial record."[142]

Barry Weber at AllMusic gave *Back for the Attack* three stars out of five, saying that it "certainly isn't Dokken's

---

142 Wikipedia, *Back for the Attack.*

greatest album, yet it remains a worthwhile listen." He praised the band for sounding "tighter than they ever have before," with frontman Don Dokken and guitarist George Lynch being "at the top of their game."[143]

While not generally placed on the same lofty height as *Under Lock and Key*, the album is nevertheless an excellent composition. However, the music suffers a bit because of the incessant touring and inner struggles that were ripping the band apart at the time. The writing and recording sessions were at times disjointed and anything but smooth. There were also times when the guys couldn't get along and had to work in separate studios, and more than one song had to go through painful rewrites. This notwithstanding, the record shows that the guys were maturing musically, particularly with tracks like "Lost Behind the Wall" and "Kiss of Death"—songs that dealt with the Cold War and AIDS; issues that were hugely relevant in 1987.

"We were doing the album on the road," commented Lynch. "We were doing the album within the tour. We weren't even there for the mixing; we were approving mixes over the phone. Coming off the previous album there were a lot of expectations from our fans and also ourselves. In retrospect, I don't think we were up to it. I think if we were able to be more hands on and weren't so inundated with touring and being as busy as we were, it might have worked, because the material was great. But I think it was ok."[144]

"Well, those sessions weren't very good," said Don. "And I don't think that's a very good album. I think there were two or three good songs, which were the singles, and there was a

---

143 Ibid
144 *Guitar World magazine*, by Gary Graff, September 1999.

lot of filler. It's a long album and there's a lot of masturbatory guitar playing. I don't think that album is very good. I think *Under Lock and Key* was our shining star. We pulled it together for that. The cocaine abuse was getting very bad for *Back for the Attack*. That's why those sessions took a lot of time. There was a lot of cocaine around."[145]

Continuing, Don went on to say, "That's when the things started with, 'I don't want Don in the studio.' I submitted my songs from my house, and they learned them and I wasn't even around for rehearsal , and I wasn't even around for the mixes either. We were already on tour with Aerosmith when they mixed it.

"I really believe if we would have stayed together, we would have done *Shadowlife* after that. It was headed there. I was already getting demands where Jeff was going to write two songs, George was going to write two songs, I wasn't allowed to write any more songs with the rest of the band.

"And I was like, 'Wait a minute, how about just the best songs should be on the record?' and George had already said to me after *Back for the Attack,* he said, 'I'm not going to make any more records with you if you get to write anymore songs than the rest of the band.' And I was like, 'Well what does it matter?' Everybody in the band was equal. It wasn't like Don Dokken gets more money or anything like that. There are a lot of bands like Bon Jovi, where they take all the money. Dokken was a four-way split. You know Mick had it made. He's the drummer, he made dollar for dollar what I made. He doesn't write any songs, he gets full publishing, full royalties and all he had to do was just be the drummer.

---

145 Popoff Archive, 3: Hair Metal, Don Dokken, By Martin Popoff, Power Chord Press 2017.

But that is the deal we made. I wanted everybody to be equal. It wasn't Don Dokken, the rock star, with you guys as sidemen."[146]

The album starts off with the power metal "Kiss of Death," a track with an aggressive opening riff that is unmistakably Lynch. From there the listener is offered up an LP that is packed full of outstanding songs. Like other Dokken records *Back for the Attack* offers plenty of variety with a hybrid of heavy melodic rockers and poppy, quasi ballads. It does not however contain the true '80s "Power Ballad."

For the album, George chose to go with a heavier yet tighter guitar sound that downright rocks. And as one would expect from a Dokken record, the album is rife with Lynch's outstanding, in your face, guitar licks and mind-bending solos.

Because the album has a heavier production than *Under Lock and Key,* Jeff's impressive bass work and Mick's thundering drums tend to stand out more. In fact, Mick's drumming is reminiscent at times of such luminaries as John Bonham and Cozy Powell. Don's vocals are spot on and as a singer he is at the absolute peak of his vocal abilities.

Like any record there are a few negatives. Some fans found the album to be a bit formulaic, while others thought that it could have done without the "fillers" like, "Heaven Sent," "So Many Tears" and "Stop Fighting Love." These weaker tracks, however, do little to diminish the overall quality of the album.

---

146 Popoff Archive, 3: Hair Metal, Don Dokken, By Martin Popoff, Power Chord Press 2017.

One outstanding feature of the record is "Mr. Scary." The song is a heavy four-minute instrumental that displays Lynch's mastery and gives the listener a mind-blowing earful of unbridled 80s shredding.

"Mr. Scary is just a collection of riffs without the soloing," explains George. At first it was intended to be a song, but George and Jeff couldn't get a melody to work with it. "But I really liked it," continues George. "And I wanted to ensure it was going to be on the record, so I had to do something with it on my own." So, during an all-night studio session George worked the riffs while using a Sustainiac device and added a healthy dose of octave effects to achieve what he calls, Mr. Scary. "The song is basically one big guitar solo. But it was done the same way I do all of my solos; I compose them, rather than just play a collection of sporadic ideas."[147]

Giving his thoughts on the album and when the serious trouble started within the band, Jeff said, "Well I know it started for Don during the making of *Back for the Attack*. I think he felt kind of on the outside, because the three of us were living in Arizona and he was living in L.A, so I know that that was part of it. But I mean, he came out to Arizona one time, that was when we sat down and did "Kiss of Death." George and I had the music and I remember being at my apartment with Don and he and I working out the lyrics.

"So, there was still some decent stuff but I think during the making of the record he started feeling a bit left out in a sense. He always kinda did anyways. To our credit he sort of separated himself in many ways. But I think he experienced it more. And then I know he was disappointed because we

---

147 *Guitar World magazine*, by Gary Graff, September 1999.

didn't have a ballad on *Back for the Attack* and that really really bothered him. And you know the song "Walk Away," which ended up coming back later on, the genesis for that song started during the *Back for the Attack* sessions while we were in the studio. And we started working on the song and it kinda got blown aside and honestly George just said 'this is no good, let's not do this.' And I know that really bothered Don, but it wasn't great what we were working on. What we should have done was work harder to make it great at the time, and I do understand Don's point that we should have worked hard to come up with a good ballad. You know it was 1987, everyone had ballads, that's what you did.

"So, there was that and I think that left a really bad taste in his mouth, I know it did because we talked about it. So I think that's when the seeds really started to grow with him. Then I think he started to look at his options in other places. *Back for the Attack* was not as cohesive a record. There was a lot of problems. There were dissention problems, there were drug problems, there were other things that happened on *Back for the Attack*."[148]

Even with the strenuous writing and recording sessions *Back for the Attack* pushed Dokken's fame to its absolute peak. They were regulars on MTV and on the covers of every popular rock magazine on the market. As a result, opportunities became available that many lesser bands were never given. One such opportunity was the chance to write a song and film a video for the movie *"A Nightmare on Elm Street Part 3: Dream Warriors."* The song, which turned out to be a big hit, was largely responsible for the album's massive success. The accompanying video, which was one

---

148 Jeff Pilson interview with James Curl.

of Dokken's best, was an instant hit on MTV and helped make Dokken a household name.

The first *Nightmare on Elm Street* made its terrifying debut on November 9, 1984. The film introduced the world to Freddy Krueger, a disfigured child killer who wields a glove affixed with razor sharp claws. The movie was an instant commercial success and spawned several frightening sequels. Robert Englund, the actor who played Freddy became hugely famous, while Freddy became an icon and kids all over the world had trouble sleeping.

"It was a great experience," said Pilson. "Our manager at the time, Cliff Burnstein, was very close with Wes Craven, who was the guy behind the whole *Nightmare on Elm Street* franchise. They were close friends. Cliff got us all a copy of the script. George and I took the script away and we just literally took lines out of it to add into the song and we delivered the song and they loved it. It was pretty damn cool. And then doing the video with Robert Englund, who plays Freddy Krueger, he is just a kick in the ass, funny guy. Just a great guy. We had a lot of fun."[149]

Pilson went on to say, "I mean, that movie got us a lot of attention. *Back for the Attack* went platinum in three weeks, so obviously it helped. You know, we had great management, we had some great people behind us. I think that's part of the leftover feeling I have for that whole period," added Pilson. "It's like, 'God, you know, we had so many opportunities and great chances. What a shame that we blew it all up and broke up.' But hey, you know, it is what it is. We had a great shot there. I think we came up with some

---

149 Jeff Pilson recalls Dokken's Nightmare on Elm Street experience with Dream Warriors, by Jeff Giles, March 7, 2018.

great music too, but even *Back for the Attack* isn't as strong as it could have been, had we been more together. That's just what happens."[150]

Continuing, Jeff said, "Not only was it a great thing to be involved in the movie, but the video that came out afterwards was the first time that a commercially released movie included a music video from the band that did the title song. That got us a lot of exposure. I would say that "Dream Warriors" was a critical song for us as far as introducing us to a lot of people, and it is a very consummate Dokken-sounding song. It sort of established our sound with a lot of people, which was a great thing."[151]

For the writing of "Dream Warriors," Don had to take a different approach. Instead of coming up with the lyrics organically, he was given a script and a guideline where the theme, chorus and title were dictated to him. "The director gave me a guideline," explained Don. "Nobody in my career had ever given me a guideline. He said, 'Look, this movie is called 'Dream Warriors' … It has to be about the darkness. It has to be about dreams. It has to be about Freddy Krueger. You have to put the words Dream Warriors in the chorus …' Everything was just dictated and I had no wiggle room. And then I had to ask the director—I hadn't seen any of the *Nightmare* movies—what's the movie about? So he sent me the script. And I went, 'OK, OK, this guy lives in people's dreams.' I wasn't into the whole monster thing by then. I wasn't into horror flicks.

---

150 Ibid
151 Jeff Pilson recalls trying to avoid Dokken's first break up by selling ideas to keep going to Don Dokken, by Joel Gausten, April 16, 2018.

"There were a million monster movies. But this was the first one about an imaginary demon that only lives in your dreams. I don't think there's a movie that's ever been done like that before. People could have seen Freddy as campy and corny. But people actually went—'he's frightening.' Everyone has nightmares. What do we try to do about nightmares? Forget about them. That song—all the lyrics were about, you go to sleep and you believe you're not alone. And like the lyric says, 'I wonder if these heavy eyes … can face the unknown.' Because no one likes nightmares."[152]

Speaking of the making of the video, Don said, "Robert Englund is a super, super sweet guy. It was fun and it was one of our biggest exorbitant, expensive things that we did. They had all the things from the movie set put away in storage, like the fake walls and the fake hell. So we went out to Simi Valley to a giant 80,000 square foot warehouse and they basically rebuilt the sets and the house. And Robert was great, you know he was in makeup and he's a sweetheart. We laughed because we were eating pizza until about ten o'clock at night and he used to wear these four panels, the burnt face with four pieces of plastic on his face. And he's eating pizza and I'm like, 'Robert, part of your face is falling off.' And they had to put some spirit gum and put it back on."[153]

Recalling his own experience while making the video, Lynch goes on to explain, "They built this elaborate horror set for us for the video. And we were in the trailers, you know they had production trailers. We're supposed to be getting ready, and Freddy was all in make-up. So he looks like he looks in 'Nightmare on Elm Street.' Which was kind of

---

152 How Dokken made it safe for me to sleep again, by Michael Friedman Ph.D.
153 Don Dokken interview with James Curl.

bizarre to be sitting there talking to a guy that looks like that you know. He had the gloves with the blades on and we were doing coke. So, he's using his blade fingers, to serve up coke to everybody. With the knife hand thing. It was kind of surreal. I mean hey, that is a long time ago, that is what everyone was doing back in the day, sorry, but it's a true story.

"I was so high during the making of that video, I couldn't bust through the wall. There is a point in my guitar solo where I am supposed to come crashing through this wall. The wall is called a breakaway wall. It's made, so that it looks like a real wall, but a fly could break through it, an infant could break through it. But I was so high and so weak I couldn't even break through it. And they had to keep re-setting up the wall, and re-shooting it because I couldn't fucking get through it. They thought, 'Oh, Lynch is buff, he'll get through that thing no problem'—which is why in the video, if you watch it, I am laughing."[154]

The video, which had scenes from the movie seamlessly edited in, is now iconic and the song has since become a Dokken classic. Robert, as Freddy does an outstanding job and was even good enough to provide a humorous ending. At the conclusion of the video, after Dokken defeats Freddy with their music, Freddy wakes up screaming revealing that the video was actually his nightmare. He then exclaims, "What a nightmare, who were those guys!?"

Even with all the success of Back for the Attack and a great video, the unhappiness within the band was growing. For the moment the guys were holding it together, albeit

---

154 Metal Sludge, George Lynch details Dokken doing cocaine off of Freddy Krueger's razor glove during the "Dream Warriors" video shoot, June 25, 2014.

barely. Having wrapped up the Aerosmith tour in February of '88, Dokken got right back on the road in March with AC/DC, but the sky was darkening and thunderclouds were gathering—things were about to go from bad to worse in a hurry.

Chapter 9
The Break Up

In March of '88 the guys headed over to the UK to play six shows with AC/DC. On one of the stops, at Wembley Stadium on March 13, things turned ugly. Throughout the day Don and George had been bickering off and on. "George was harassing me every day," recalls Don, "just fucking with me and threatening me and trying to get violent."[155]

Their arguments finally reached a breaking point in the back seat of a limo when George erupted with anger. "He jumped me," said Don. "And he just leaned over and got me in a head lock and he started squeezing my neck—like squeezing to break my neck—and I was just punching him in the face and we just went at it. The disappointment was that Jeff just sat there, Mick just sat there and my road manger just sat there. Nobody intervened, they just sat there and watched and I thought, 'Well, I know where your guys' loyalties lie.' "[156]

Speaking of the incident, Jeff said, "The European tour we did with AC/DC, there were some really bad moments there. The infamous fist fight in the limousine. We were in London on the way to the show at Wembley Arena and fists came out in a moving car, and everyone got hit. And we stopped the car and then of course it cooled down, but tensions were really bad. And then of course on the Monsters of Rock tour it got really bad."[157]

As the limo arrived at the venue, Don and George were still threatening each other and their fighting spirits were ablaze. Intent on continuing their fisticuffs in the parking lot, their road manager stepped in as car doors swung open and said, "Guys! You're on in ten minutes!" With the realization

---

155 Don Dokken interview with James Curl.
156 Ibid.
157 Jeff Pilson interview with James Curl.

that they had to be on stage, the two combatants looked at each other, shrugged and walked in as if nothing had happened. "When I went on stage," said Don, "there was a line on George's side of the stage and he said, 'if you cross it during the show I'll smash my guitar over your head.' That's the way it went in front of 18,000 people the rest of the night."[158]

With the AC/DC tour finished in March of '88 the guys headed over to Japan during April where they played shows in Tokyo, Osaka and Nagoya. Speaking of the tour, Pilson remarked, "It was noteworthy in that it was our last touring together in the '80s where there was still a band vibe."[159]

While in Japan some of their shows were recorded and compiled onto the live album titled *Beast from the East* which was released on November 16, 1988. The album features live versions of the band's most popular songs and biggest hits. In addition it also included a new studio track called, "Walk Away"—essentially the missing ballad that never made it on *Back for the Attack*.

The album earned the band their only Grammy Award nomination in 1990 for Best Metal Performance, losing to Metallica's "One." The honor, however went largely unnoticed by the guys. "I was excited, personally," said Jeff. "It seemed like a great honor to me. But we were so untogether that there was very little recognition that we had really done anything. It just didn't feel like a band at that point. It was kinda like, 'Oh, really? Now we get a Grammy? …it doesn't matter.' "[160]

A month after the Japan tour, in late May of 1988, the guys headed out on the biggest tour of their career—the Monsters of Rock.

The traveling festival kicked off on May 23 in East Troy, Wisconsin at the Alpine Valley Music Theatre. Van Halen,

---

158 20 questions with Don Dokken.
159 Ibid.
160 Jeff Pilson interview with James Curl.

supporting their *OU812* album, co-headlined the massive event with the Scorpions, followed by Metallica, Dokken and Kingdom Come. It was certainly an impressive line-up of big names especially for a one-day event and proved to be extremely popular. However, things didn't start off smoothly. And as one might imagine, running such a massive event presented its share of problems.

"At the opening night of the tour the sound quality during Dokken's set was poor and as a result the band was booed heavily by attendees. A lighting rig fell during the Scorpions' set, and Sammy Hagar fell off the stage. The amphitheater at Alpine Valley had been recently sodded and before the Scorpions took the stage, fans had become impatient and started hurling chunks of the freshly laid sod into the air. Attendants came out and threatened to close down the venue. The scene then calmed down and the show finished without further problem."[161]

From there the bands continued on across America playing to huge crowds in sold out stadiums. But for the guys in Dokken things were getting bad. What should have been one of the highlights of Dokken's collective career turned out to be, "Best times, worst times," reflected Don. "We played for a million people in four weeks, playing with Van Halen, Scorpions, Metallica, but yet the band was absolutely out of their minds on cocaine and alcohol.

"I warned them. We had been on the road for 18 months. It was the biggest tour we ever did. We were gone 18 months, nonstop. It was a nightmare. We were really tired. By the time we hit Monsters to wrap it up, we were just exhausted. I kept begging and pleading for someone—Jeff, Mick, the management, the label—to talk to George and tell him to stop it. Just like Monsters of Rock, he had this thing where he'd go behind the amps and play his solos and hide because the roadie's holding a straw while he snorts coke while he's

---

161 Wikipedia, Monsters of Rock tour, 1988.

playing. When you're doing that in front of 100,000 people and cameras are on the stage ... it's very unprofessional. I thought it hurt the band."[162]

Moreover, Don said that the band's performances at Monsters of Rock were made weaker by the other members' drug use. "We just sucked. Those guys were sloppy, hungover."[163]

Despite what should have been a great time, Dokken was crumbling faster than a building that had been hit with dynamite. "Yeah, at the Monsters of Rock I knew we had nowhere to go but down. The band was completely imploding," said Don. To try and help with the growing problems, the band brought in a counselor. "We actually brought out a counselor," said Don, "the same counselor that counseled Aerosmith. He basically said, 'you guys are doomed.' "[164]

It wasn't just drug use that was affecting the shows. George, who was unhappy with some of the things that Don had said, began to act out in frustration. He would sabotage Dokken's performances by playing with his back to the audience or playing out of sight altogether. Other times he would walk off stage when the band was supposed to do an encore. "Twice," said Don, "during the tour, he walked off on the encore. We would have a huge encore; 80,000 people would give us an encore, and I came back on stage and announced the song, 'In My Dreams' and I turn around and made the cue, and I looked behind the stage and George is walking like 100 yards off to his dressing room holding his guitar. Shit like that will kill you."[165]

The guitarist blamed his behavior on Don, claiming that Don had planned to break up the band before Monsters of Rock and that the singer had told them, "I'm gonna try to

---

162 In his own words, Don Dokken talks all things Dokken, March 12, 2015.
163 Ibid.
164 Don Dokken interview with James Curl.
165 Popoff Archive, 3: Hair Metal, Don Dokken, by Martin Popoff.

take the whole thing and run with it, and you guys are gonna get left in the dust, and if you're lucky, I might hire you."[166] George also claimed that Don said, "I'm not gonna tour with you guys after this. If you're not gonna give me the name, I'm gonna sue you. And maybe you guys could work for me. I could hire you."[167] George says that this left him feeling, "completely demoralized" on the tour.

According to George, Don's threats of a break-up marked the beginning of the end for Dokken, and as Lynch confessed during an interview, "That backfired on all of us. Financially, it backfired on all of us, 'cause we didn't get that massive (deal). At that point, I think, that year Mötley Crüe got a $25 million deal, Anthrax got a $12.5 million deal. We would have been fine. Basically, we had a lot of leverage. We were gonna be a free agent, so it was really a shame. It just didn't go right for anybody."[168]

Additionally, George placed the blame squarely on Don's shoulders for the final breakup of the group, saying, "If you have a record deal, or a master deal, for a certain amount of time, and you have increasing record sales, and then you get to the point where the deal ends, your managers come in and renegotiate and you get paid. Then you're set for life—possibly. That's when everything changes. That's what you worked for, for those however many years... Everything you've invested in time and energy, you get paid back for.

---

166 *Ultimate Classic Rock*, George Lynch blames Dokken's break up on Don Dokken's greed, by Jeff Giles, December 4, 2014.
167 Dokken: The Hair Metal Band that Hated Itself, by Paul Elliot, October 2, 2015
168 *Ultimate Classic Rock*, George Lynch blames Dokken's break up on Don Dokken's greed, by Jeff Giles, December 4, 2014.

And the singer, at that point, decided that he wanted it all, he didn't wanna share it with us, and he let us know that."[169]

Because of George's behavior, things got so bad that some of the members from other bands took it upon themselves to talk to the guitarist. "Oh, yeah," said Don. "I remember Monsters of Rock. It's sad but Eddie Van Halen, Rudolph Schenker and Lars Ulrich, they all went to George and said, 'what are you doing?' I mean they came to his room and it was embarrassing. I remember Eddie Van Halen knocking on George's door saying, 'you know, you have to change yourself, George.' And George said, 'I can't help it, I hate Don. I hate Don's guts and I can't do it. How did you do it?' Eddie would say, 'Look, I didn't like David Lee Roth. We fought like cats and dogs, but nobody knew about it on stage. We didn't wash our laundry on stage. For an hour-and-a-half a night we're the best of friends because we owed it to our fans.'

"And that came from Eddie, who George really respected. And I thought cool! Now he's going to go out there and kick ass. And he went out there the next night and played the entire show with his back to the audience. And when I announced him for his guitar solo, the spotlight went on him and he was standing behind an amplifier hiding. I was so humiliated and embarrassed that I went and bought a bottle of Jack Daniels and just got completely shit-faced."[170]

Besides band drama there were other factors that affected the shows as well. According to Don, they didn't stand a chance playing second to Metallica. "Oh, man," groaned

---

169 *Blabbermouth.net*, George Lynch says Don Dokken's greed caused break up of Dokken's classic line up, December 3, 2014.
170 Exclusive! Kirby interview with vocalist Don Dokken, by Jeff Kirby, December 2, 2004.

Don. "After Metallica went out and played *Master of Puppets*, we sounded like the fucking Partridge Family."[171]

Don asked his co-manager Cliff Burnstein if the two bands could switch places. "I told him, 'I know we're making twice the money as Metallica, but can you please put 'em on after us? Because they're killing us.' "[172] Burnstein said no.

Following a show in New York, Don's humiliation was sealed by a scathing review. "There was this huge review in the New York Times," said Don. "It said that Van Halen kicked ass, the Scorpions were super-amazing, Metallica are the new upstarts just breaking out in America, Kingdom Come was good… and there was just one line about us. It said, 'During Dokken's set a record number of hotdogs were sold.' It was horrible."[173]

With the band falling apart, the pressure was getting to Don. The singer began suffering anxiety attacks, and was self-medicating with Valium and alcohol. Right or wrong, he put the blame on George for the terrible mess that the band was in.

"Well," said Don. "I was taking tranquilizers and anti-anxiety medication. I went through a stint where I was actually having heart palpitations. I was waking up and my heart was racing. I called the doctor and wanted to know what the hell was going on. It ended up that he said I was suffering from major, major hyper anxiety. The doctor was a really good friend of mine, and he actually came on the road a few times to witness what was taking place on the road. I was like, 'I can't explain it to you, you have to go on the road to understand this.' Afterwards he said, 'It's too bad. You guys are doing so well, but it's like you're in a den of thieves. It's like your trying to watch your wallet every five seconds.'

---

171 Dokken: The Hair Metal Band that Hated Itself, by Paul Elliot, October 2, 2015.
172 Ibid.
173 Ibid.

It was pretty obvious that there was no love lost between any of us."[174]

On July 30, 1988, Dokken played their final show on the Monsters of Rock tour. Having reached his breaking point, Don called a meeting with the band, management and senior figures at Elektra to deliver an ultimatum. "I said I couldn't continue to play with Lynch. I told Jeff and Mick that we could continue, but that George and I had come to a crossroads. This is over."

"On the last day of the Monsters of Rock tour we had management, record company [people] and accountants and everybody fly out to a big meeting in Denver," explains Jeff. "Our last show was at Mile High stadium in Denver and everybody came from the East Coast and the West Coast to have this big meeting. We had the meeting in a boardroom in the hotel right across from Mile High stadium at the top floor. And in that meeting they discussed us staying together and the label offered us a million dollars for our live record, which was a lot of money for a live record at the time. And they were trying to give us incentive to stay together."[175]

Knowing that Dokken was on the verge of bigger success and was a viable money maker, Elektra made additional attempts to keep the guys together. "They offered $10 million to do two more albums," Don says. "That's a lot of frickin' money."[176] However, Jeff and Mick decided to stick with George. "That's when I left the band. It was almost impossible, since it was my band. And who wants to walk away from a lucrative career? But if I hadn't, I probably would have had a nervous breakdown."[177]

Jeff, however, felt that the band should have remained together and that the best was yet to come.

---

174 Exclusive! Kirby interview with vocalist Don Dokken, by Jeff Kirby, December 2, 2004.
175 Jeff Pilson interview with James Curl.
176 Dokken: The Hair Metal Band that Hated Itself, by Paul Elliot, October 2, 2015
177 Ibid.

"I remember having many talks with Don," explained Jeff. "I would pull out statistics, like, only 41 albums went Platinum in 1988, and we were one of them! I was really trying to sell the idea of keeping the band together for at least a couple more cycles. Our management was trying to do the same, they were dangling large monetary carrots in front of us. Money was one of the reasons that I thought we should stay together, but I also felt like, No! We haven't taken this as far as we could. In retrospect, having broken up probably eliminated us from being part of the carnage that 'hair metal' received in the early '90s, we were already gone by then.

"We did have a career after that; we were able to come back a couple of times. That may or may not have happened had we continued on. Who knows? But I did not want the band to break up; I did think we had more to do. I thought had we done one more record, we would have really put ourselves in a much, much bigger position—which again, would have suffered terribly in the '90s, but maybe we would have had a better springboard to jump off from there."[178]

Although at this point Dokken was in the process of breaking up, the guys were still contractually obligated to do a video for the single, "Walk Away." Despite the song being written while the band was in a state of turmoil, the melodic ballad is beautifully composed and ranks among Dokken's best love songs. Don's vocals are exceptional throughout the track and his lyrics evoke feelings of longing and lost love, while George's guitar solo is emotionally charged and eloquently epic. For the kids of the '80s, who grew up with the song, hearing it today no doubt conjures memories of first loves, broken hearts and tearful goodbyes.

The song was accompanied by a music video, which featured members of the band performing atop the picturesque Santa Monica Mountains overlooking Topanga Canyon and the Pacific Ocean.

---

178 *Sleaze Roxx,* Jeff Pilson recalls trying to avoid Dokken first breaking up, April 16, 2018.

"A friend of Don's, a guy by the name of Louie was the heir to the S&H Green Stamps fortune and he had 15,000 acres out in Topanga Canyon," said Jeff. "And he lived in this very bizarre eccentric house, which you can see in the 'Walk Away' video—just a very strange, strange house. He was a very odd guy, but a really nice guy and friends with a lot of people. That's how I managed to get George Harrison's autograph, he was friends with George Harrison, and Don was up there when George was there and Don very kindly asked George for an autograph for me. But just a really bizarre place.

"And the live scenes that we were playing were in this kinda like mini amphitheater slash ritual pit that had actually been used by the Manson family (that's Charles Manson, the notorious cult leader). They had actually done sacrifices, they weren't human sacrifices I don't believe, but you could actually see stains of animal blood on parts of the place we were playing. And that's what was overlooking the whole coast and Malibu and it was a bizarre place and an interesting video. So, technically we weren't broken up yet and we had the obligation of doing the *Beast from the East* record, but we all knew inside that we were broken up."[179]

With the filming of the video completed, the guys went their separate ways, and by March of 1989, Dokken was officially broken up. However, the acrimonious split didn't mean that the battle was over, in fact it had just begun. On his own, Don tried to reform a new Dokken, and George, Jeff and Mick promptly filed a lawsuit. After the litigation proceedings the judge ruled in their favor and Don was prohibited from using the Dokken name. "We had a contract that we signed in 1984," explained Jeff, "that made it very clear that you couldn't leave the band then take the name. No matter who you were."[180]

---

[179] Jeff Pilson interview with James Curl.
[180] Ibid.

"Unfortunately," says Don, "I did send a paper saying, 'If you're gonna stay with George, I'm out.' The judge ruled in their favor, and I wasn't allowed to use the name Dokken for five years. That hurt me." Furthermore, Don said, "I never realized that I could lose my name. I never thought that they could go to court and take my birthright."[181]

"It got mildly ugly but nothing really horrible," said Jeff recalling the lawsuit. "We did the lawsuit mostly through depositions and we got a judgment so Don couldn't call his thing Dokken. He could call it Don Dokken all he wanted. And then we moved on."[182]

Although the guys may have "moved on" things were far from over for Dokken. And like an old fighter that can't resist the lure of the ring, there would be a couple of comebacks.

---

[181] Don Dokken interview with James Curl.
[182] Jeff Pilson interview with James Curl.

Chapter 10
Up from the Ashes
and Lynch Mob

With Dokken completely splintered, the guys looked to regroup. Don embarked on a solo career, while George and Mick decided to stick together and form Lynch Mob. Jeff, who had seen the writing on the wall, had already put together a band called Flesh and Blood with fellow musicians Vinny Appice, Randy Hansen and Michael Diamond. His original intention, however was to get George and Mick to join his band, but instead they opted to go the Lynch Mob route.

"I didn't join Lynch Mob because I had already formed Flesh and Blood," said Jeff. "My initial hope was that George and Mick would join me in that. But they didn't want to do that, so I carried on."[183]

Being proficient with multiple instruments Jeff handled lead vocals, rhythm guitar and keyboards. Together the guys recorded a number of songs with the help of engineer Angelo Arcuri and Neil Kernon, who stepped in to help mix the recordings. Unfortunately, their band name was stolen, which forced Jeff to change the name to War and Peace.

"I had been working with a guy by the name of Michael Diamond," said Jeff, "and he and I and Vinny Appice and a guitar player by the name of Randy Hanson had a band called Flesh and Blood and we, I believe it was the fall of '88, we went in and started recording demos, which became the *Flesh and Blood Sessions*. So that's what I did right away. That evolved over time into War and Peace, because somebody stole the name Flesh and Blood from me, and so we changed to War and Peace and it took a long time. We

---

183 Jeff Pilson interview with James Curl.

waited until Vinny left Dio before we really did anything and then by that time the scene was changing. So I waited too long, absolutely."[184]

"The band that took the name Flesh and Blood," explained Jeff, "was previously called Dear Mr. President. They were rehearsing down the hall from Flesh and Blood while we were working up what became "The Flesh and Blood Sessions." The real irony is that the producer for Dear Mr. President, who became Flesh and Blood, was Mick Jones."[185] (Guitarist for the band Foreigner, a band in which Jeff would eventually become a member).

The adoption of a new name was then followed by a change in line-up as well. Jeff would eventually release a total of four War and Peace albums utilizing several different members over the years. First came 1993's *Time Capsule,* featuring Russ Parrish (now the guitarist for the infamous Steel Panther), Tommy "Hendrix" Henriksen, and Ricky Parent. In 1999, Jeff released the original *Flesh & Blood Sessions.* After that came *Light at the End of the Tunnel* in 2001. In 2004, Jeff also released *The Walls Have Eyes* featuring Michael Frowein on drums and Bartholomew Toff on percussions. Jeff handled everything else.

With Flesh and Blood/War and Peace having fizzled out by late 1990, Jeff looked for other ways to pay the bills. "At some point in '91 I played on the last MSG record, then in late '91 or early '92 I ended up doing an acoustic tour with them and played a 12 string guitar. It was just Robin, Michael and myself on the road which was really fun."[186] From there Jeff worked as a session musician with Wild Horses.

While Jeff was occupied with his projects, George and Mick had formed Lynch Mob along with vocalist Oni Logan and bass player Anthony Esposito. Together the quartet were

---

184 Ibid.
185 Ibid
186 Ibid.

hard at work on their first highly anticipated album, *Wicked Sensation.*

Reflecting on putting Lynch Mob together, George said, "Well, when I put Lynch Mob together in 1989, I wanted to put my dream band together. I had my pick of the litter; I had people beating down my door, just about anybody in the band. The idea was – there was not going to be any excuses with this band. With Dokken, if I made my perfect band, I wouldn't have picked Don for my lead singer. He came from blues, roots and r&b music. I come from hard rock and '60s rock, which is all derivative of blues and r&b obviously. Don wasn't really the singer for the music I was hearing in my head. I'm not saying it isn't good music, it's just not my cup of tea.

"I think what happened actually, with Dokken, is because of that we had a very strange but successful chemistry. I brought what I described to you to the table, and Don brought what he did to the table, which is the antithesis of what I did. That's what created this chemistry, which people recognized and appreciated. With Lynch Mob, there wasn't any of that. With Lynch Mob, I did what I went with, what I felt I wanted with no apologies. We get a very bluesy, kind of Paul Rodgers' style singer who comes from an Aretha Franklin blues/r&b/gospel camp. That's what I wanted to hear. So, we created this little greasier, dirtier, harder-edged thing. That's always what I wanted; that's my core musical impulse, it is where gravity draws me, that's my foundation and I've always tried to keep that solid as a foundational core band."[187]

Having his pick of the litter so to speak, George decided to go with a hot young singer named Oni Logan. Oni was basically unknown on an international level at the time, but had made a big name for himself on the Sunset Strip and George certainly found a gem.

---

187 *CrypticRock.com,* George Lynch interview, December 18, 2017.

Born in Buenos Aires, Argentina, Oni immigrated to the United States when he was 11 months old, eventually settling in Stanford, Connecticut. Oni's father found work in a factory that made rivets for airplanes that were used in the Vietnam War. The Logan family eventually relocated to South Florida when Oni was nine. The young boy found Florida to be a land of adventure and described his childhood as a "Huckleberry Finn kind of lifestyle... Jumping off bridges, exploring the canals, and being with alligators and catfish. I was one of those kids that ran around with shorts on, barefoot, no shirt on kind of kid."[188]

The young singer got his start as lead vocalist for the band Diamond Rose in South Florida, gigging with them from 1985 to 1987. That band consisted of Dave Rhodes (guitar), Mike D'Amico (drums), Marc Wolpert (bass), and Mark "Smitty" Smith (guitar).

Diamond Rose became well-known in South Florida, but Oni left to join another Florida-based band by the name of Defiance. After a year of fronting the band, Marc Ferrari the guitarist for Keel invited Oni to Los Angeles to become the singer for his new band Ferrari. At the same time Ferrari was starting to get serious, Oni was invited to join Racer X in a new incarnation that included all the original members except star guitarist Paul Gilbert. Paul had at this point left to form Mr. Big. Oni accepted the offer to sing for Racer X, however after just one show the members decided to go their separate ways at which point Oni regrouped with Ferrari for a short stint.

"I was doing some shows with them," said Oni, "and what had happened was George Lynch and Mick Brown just came out of Dokken and they were looking for a singer for their new project. And they went up to the first person that might be able to help them and it was Juan Alderete from Racer X. And they said, who's the new cat in town named Oni Logan?

---

188 The Double Stop Podcast, Ep.31, Oni Logan.

So they seeked me out, they came to a Whisky show and they put all plans on me, and offered me all this bunch of money. You know it wasn't about the money for me, because I had no conceptual idea about money, I was just a young dude who just like wanted to be a rock 'n' roll guy, ya know. What I wanted was the chemistry, that's how it's always been with me, because I come from a classic rock background. I come from Fog Hat, I come from Led Zeppelin, I come from Deep Purple, I come from Pink Floyd, I come from Cream, all the good stuff when bands got together in a room and they made music and that's what I was into and George was into that idea. And that's why I ended up going with them because he was so passionate about it."[189]

Wicked Sensation was unleashed to the public on October 23, 1990 and was a far cry from what George had done with his former band. The music was a bit heavier and exuded a bluesy vibe as well as a groovier hard rock sound similar to what Badlands was doing at the time. Although Lynch Mob has an entirely different sound and feel than Dokken, it didn't steer clear of the hair metal formula entirely. Tracks like, "River of Love," "Bed of Roses" and "For a Million Years" have definite hair Metal-esque moments and would have done well in 1986.

As one might expect, the album is overflowing with Lynch's guitar-driven fury that is at times absolutely fever pitched, especially on the track "Sweet Sister Mercy." Another nice touch to the album is a bit of a swaggering Southern rock influence. The song "Sweet Sister Mercy" even has Oni blowing a harmonica, which fits perfectly with the song.

Upon its release the album garnered a lot of positive reviews from fans and critics alike, and is considered one of Lynch's finest compositions, with many fans deeming it a highlight of the guitarist's illustrious career. From the album

---

189 Ibid

came two successful singles, "River Of Love" climbing to the 19 spot on Billboard's Mainstream Rock chart as well as "Wicked Sensation" which reached 31.

While his ex-bandmates were busy with their respective projects, Don had assembled his own supergroup of formidable musicians. To handle guitar duties, shredders John Norum of Europe fame and Billy White formerly of the progressive Metal band Watchtower were brought in. This gave the band a powerful dual-guitar power plant. Seated at the skins was Mikkey Dee formerly of King Diamond and future Motörhead. To fill in on bass, Don called on old friend Peter Baltas, whom he considered the best bassist he ever played with.

Remembering how he was recruited into the band, Peter said, "Well, Don was putting a band together and he had Mikkey Dee from King Diamond and John Norum and Billy White. I left Accept at the time and Don found out and he gave me a call and said he's putting this band together. That was the height of MTV and I was here in Pennsylvania and I didn't have anything to do—I just came off a world tour. So I flew over the morning after my son was born. I spent two months in Los Angeles with Don recording the album. Great White had their rehearsal room in there and they were always hanging around. Don then asked me if I wanted to join the band and I said yes, and I packed up everything here and we moved to California."[190]

Speaking of the guitar team of John and Billy and the band's chemistry Peter went on to explain, "John has a lot of Thin Lizzy and Gary Moore influence, they were two different worlds, him and Billy White. And actually Bill could play just as good as Stevie Ray Vaughn. He was from

---

190 Peter Baltas interview with James Curl.

Austin, Texas, so you know he was the new prodigy kid from down there. And that band Watchtower he had, if you listen to old albums it sounds like Stevie Ray Vaughn. So when those two worlds came together with those two players it was just magic, it really was. And it was one of the best rhythm sections there was between me and Mikkey, and then together with John and Billy and Don's great vocals it was a kick ass band."[191]

With such an impressive arsenal of instrumental firepower at his disposal, Don and company set about creating an album. The result turned out to be the aptly titled, *Up from the Ashes,* which was released on October 21, 1990. The album is melodic heavy metal at its finest and was more representative of the kind of rock 'n' roll that Don wanted to play, much the same way *Wicked Sensation* represented George's musical personality.

Following the release, the guys headed out on a short tour in the States then over to Japan. Remembering the time Peter said, "We toured Japan and the States and everything was great, back then it was called dial MTV and the video "Mirror, Mirror" was really high up there and we had high hopes."[192]

The music videos for the songs "Stay" and "Mirror Mirror" received moderate airplay on MTV's *Headbanger's Ball.* Nevertheless, the album did not achieve the commercial success attained by previous Dokken releases, but it did reach the Top 50 on the *Billboard* 200 album chart in the US.

After the tour Don decided to take his family and the band on a Hawaiian vacation. However, on the last night of their stay Don was viciously attacked by a jealous madman wielding a 2x4.

---

191 Ibid
192 Ibid.

"Well, he came in the room, I couldn't defend myself. I had my son with me, and his mother at the time. My son was like two, and it was bizarre. He came in the room, he worked at the hotel, so he had a passkey, and I didn't have the latch chain on. I don't remember much. I just remember the door opening and it's dark, and I just heard this guy yelling; 250 pound Hawaiian dude, and he had a 2 x 4, and he started swinging at the bed, and he started hitting me. And I rolled over on top of Tyler, because I didn't want his skull crushed. And I laid on top of Tyler, and his mother screaming for the lights. She's yelling call the operator, call the police, and this guy's hitting me; hitting me across the back, like nine, ten times, until the board actually broke. So I'm lucky. If I would've been hit in the head, I would've been dead, I would've had a crushed skull.

"And it was a big debacle. I was there with the Don Dokken band, and he ran out the door, I'm all bloody, and I chase him down the hallway, and cops come up and arrest me. And I said, 'What the fuck is going on?' And they say, 'Well the guy who works here, they caught him on the beach, walking down the beach, and they caught him and arrested him. And the guy said, 'Well, that guy raped my girlfriend.' And I went, 'raped his girlfriend?' Yeah, with the kids and his mother in the room. And I said 'give me my dime, I'm calling California.' It was our last night in Hawaii and what it turned out was, it was Mikkey Dee, (whom the guy was after).

"He just picked a room at random. He could've picked Billy's, John Norum, Billy White, or Mikkey Dee. So, he came into my room and just pummeled the shit out of me, and my arm, I lost all of the feelings in my hand for five years. The girl describes me as 5' 4" with a heavy Swedish accent, and I'm 6' 1" and I say 'dude.' And I said 'Wait a minute.' And the cops went to Mikkey's room and he said, 'Yes, I fucked her.' The girl is a slut, and she slept with all the tourists and that was the end of that. But the bummer is, yeah, I got hurt. And I was in therapy for three years. I still have no feeling in my left hand. All my fingers are numb. It's permanent. So I've got soft tissue damage, and I've had three back surgeries."[193]

Although *Up from the Ashes* was well-made, some fans were put off by the polished production which sounded tamer when compared to Dokken's previous studio release *"Back for the Attack."* A couple of radio friendly, lighter rockers like, "Living a Lie," "Stay" and "Mirror, Mirror" certainly didn't give the old school Dokken fans a reason to cheer. However, the LP has its share of hard rockers like, "Up from the Ashes," "Crash and Burn," "Give it Up," "Down in Flames" and "The Hunger." These songs are crammed full of great vocals, pounding rhythms and enough superlative guitar playing to make any Dokken fan happy.

As one would expect from a Don Dokken fronted band there is a proper "Power Ballad," and what a ballad. "When Love Finds A Fool" was co-written by Glenn Hughes, who also provided backing vocals. The song is a moving composition with Don sharing his feelings and Billy playing an incredibly touching and emotional guitar solo.

When asked what he thought of the album Peter replied, "I think it's an excellent album to be quite honest, I really do. And to this day the quality of songs and the caliber of the playing within the band was incredible and Don was on top of his vocal abilities back then. There were excellent songs. I still listen to it once in a while because it was well-done; I have to say one of the best albums I ever played on, love it. Almost every song was great. And this one was actually very heavy too, it had some heavy components because of the players too. Mikkey is a totally different player than Mick Brown, he is a Metal player. Billy White is one of the most gifted guitar players I ever came in contact with. If you listen

---

193 Don Dokken interview with Martin Popoff, May 2, 2008.

to the ballad "When Love Finds a Fool"… that solo on there is incredible."[194]

"I felt pressured," said Don speaking of the album. "Here I'd come out of this world-famous band, and now the band's broken up. There were some legalities—I couldn't use my last name. It was a legal issue. *Up from the Ashes* should have been released as Dokken, but I couldn't, so I had to call it Don Dokken. It wasn't a solo album; it was just another incarnation of Dokken.

"It was a great album, and an awesome band, one of my faves maybe my favorite. It's sad Geffen didn't promote it, but they were caught up in Nirvana and Guns N' Roses. They saw *Up from the Ashes* as Old School.[195]

"The guitar playing with John Norum and Billy White is just fucking amazing," said Don "The guitar playing is underrated shredding, not just John Norum, but Billy was nineteen years old when we did that record and that guy was on fire. My only regret about that record is I think it's too wet, too much reverb and stuff, it lacks some punch. I would love to get those master tapes and remix *Up from the Ashes* and dry it up a little bit and take all the reverb off of it. I think we were trying to go for a Def Leppard sound and we failed. But musically the songs are really good. The harmonies, the solos, the playing—It was just a fucking solid record. I guarantee if *Up from the Ashes* came out as a Dokken album it would probably have went gold or platinum, but Don Dokken was considered a solo album so it fell by the wayside."[196]

---

194 Peter Baltas interview with James Curl.
195 Ibid.
196 Ibid.

Continuing, Don went on to say, "It's timing. That album came out right when the whole grunge thing was hitting, and the musical styles were changing. I had done what I thought was a classic, straight-up rock 'n' roll record, and I think we got a little stigmatized —'Oh, Dokken, '80s guys, they're a hair band.' I hate that term, 'hair band.' So we kind of just couldn't survive the change in taste.

"It did good—sold almost half a million copies—but it didn't sell multi-platinum like the previous Dokken records, and the reason we didn't continue was because I got despondent. I just felt like, 'The hell with it.' I put a lot of blood and sweat and tears into that record, and I just figured, 'What's the point?' So I took a break. We all kind of went our separate ways."[197]

"I don't recall who left first," said Peter. "I think it was Mikkey. I went back with Accept and John ended up doing a couple of solo records that I played on, but he went back to Europe eventually and Don started doing Dokken again."[198]

While the ex-members of Dokken were releasing their respective albums, the musical landscape was changing rapidly. As quickly as the Sunset Strip bands had risen, they just as quickly came crashing down into a pile of neon-colored guitars and leopard print spandex. Hard rock and heavy metal was losing its grip on the public and gasping for air.

There's been a lot written about the demise of hair metal. Typically its death is blamed on the rise of grunge. To be sure, grunge certainly helped, but there were really several reasons for its fall and it wasn't just Nirvana's fault. Nor did the genre disappear entirely.

---

197 *SleazeRoxx,* Don Dokken states his 1990 *Up from the Ashes* solo album should have been a Dokken album, March 9, 2018.
198 Ibid.

By the late '80s, the L.A music scene, particularly glam and hair metal, had reached a critical saturation point. Lesser talented copycat bands had sprung up everywhere and an industry that was already overflowing with hair bands had become diluted. This caused a decline in the quality of music and a lessening of interest with fans who actually knew what good music was.

Moreover, fans that grew up in the '80s listening to bands like Dokken, Ratt and Mötley Crüe were getting older, settling down, and starting families. With the realities of making a living and paying bills, the majority of fans became turned off by the excessive and rampant hedonism of the "Decade of Decadence." As a result their interest declined. Furthermore, many of the '80s bands, like their fans, were maturing. They were wiping off the mascara, throwing away the cans of Aqua Net and giving up the spandex.

To add to the problems that were crippling many of the L.A. bands, grunge and alternative rock were starting to gain momentum, and so was rap. As a result, the overall popularity of hard rock, particularly hair metal was sent reeling. In September of 1991 Nirvana's *Nevermind* hit the public and helped slam the lid down on the hair metal coffin. The skyrocketing popularity of this new style of music was due in large part because the younger generation, like the one before, wanted their own music—a music that would define their era.

By 1993 bands that once ruled the airwaves were out. MTV and FM radio were suddenly overrun with Nirvana, Pearl Jam, Collective Soul, Jane's Addiction, Sound Garden, and Alice in Chains as well as a multitude of rap and hip-hop groups. The fun, carefree decade that was all about "Nothing but a Good Time" was regrettably and irrevocably over.

What followed was the next phase of musical evolution. It was a period that brought us a multitude of bands that were undeniably talented, yet had a completely different demeanor—not to mention a different look. Out was the big hair, make-up and bandanas; in came the ripped jeans, Doc Martin boots and thrift store flannel shirts.

And it wasn't just the image that changed. The lyrical content was decisively melancholy. To be fair, many a heavy metal song spoke of negative topics. Conversely, most of the bands from the '80s were geared towards fun and sexuality. The '90s bands were an entirely different beast. Instead of singing about "Girls, Girls, Girls" many of these new bands were all about darker lyrical subjects such as: social alienation, self-doubt, abuse, neglect, betrayal, social and emotional isolation, psychological trauma and a desire for freedom.

Despite the inexorable change that was happening to music and the decline of hair bands, there was still some juice left in rock 'n' roll. A certain kind of boogie/blues based hard rock had been on the way back ever since Guns N' Roses, The Cult and The Black Crowes broke out. These newer bands were helping keep rock 'n' roll alive, and as we shall see, despite the pummeling it was taking, rock was far from dead.

The Black Crowes' debut *Shake Your Money Maker* reached No. 4 in 1990. Skid Row released *Slave to the Grind,* in June of 1991, which went number 1. Cinderella toned down the glam thing and released the blues inspired *Heart Break Station* in November of 1990. The album climbed the charts to 19 and went platinum. Hair band Firehouse released their self-titled debut *Firehouse* in 1990. The album was met with much critical acclaim, spawned four singles and went double platinum. Metallica released *The Black Album* in 1991 and received widespread praise. It debuted at number one in ten countries and spent four consecutive weeks at the top of the *Billboard* 200, making it Metallica's first album to top album charts. It also became the band's best-selling album. And all of this happened during the grunge era.

Giving his own thoughts on the fall of the '80s bands, Don said, "I think '80s rock killed '80s rock. I think somewhere along the line it shifted from an emphasis on the music to how good does our makeup or hair or spandex look? Not to say that all of the bands that came out when we did didn't have a look, but the music was always first and foremost. Somewhere along the line it all got watered down and MTV played a huge part in that for every band, they were like 'Okay, this is what we want…everybody's gotta look like a cross between Mötley Crüe and Poison.' The videos and the visuals became so incredibly important to the suits that it was like 'Hey, wait a minute, what about the songs?' Bands started losing their edge or putting out bad songs and people didn't like them, the other bands were making better songs. I truly believe that the demise of that music was brought on by the bands themselves."[199]

Despite the shift in musical taste and the beating that rock 'n' roll was enduring, Jeff, George and Mick continued to carry on into the '90s. Don on the other hand decided to go on hiatus for a few years. Unhappy with the change in the

199 Legendary Rock Interviews, Don Dokken talks early days, acoustic shows and much more, by John Parks, December 7, 2012.

music scene and disappointed that *Up From the Ashes* didn't do better, he focused his attention on other passions. "I got my black belt in Korea from Grandmaster Kim, head of the Taekwondo Federation, it took many years," said Don. "I also spent time during those years building a recording studio, producing albums, building a house and spending time with my kids—basically I was retired. After 10 years of non-stop touring it was time for a break."[200]

And like most breaks, especially for bands, they come to an end and Dokken would soon be on the comeback trail.

---

200 Don Dokken interview with James Curl.

Chapter 11
Dysfunctional
and Shadowlife

It was while Don was on his extended break that he began feeling the itch to do some writing. So he called Jeff.

"I started working with Don in the spring of '92," said Jeff. "I remember he called me up out of the blue and he said, 'Hey, do you want to write?' and he had done a solo record at that point and it had been a disappointment for him; he thought it should have done better. And so he asked me if I wanted to write and I said 'yeah, sure.' And I had just been on the road with MSG playing an acoustic tour with them. And we got together and we started writing and in the next several months we wrote the bulk of what was the *Dysfunctional* record. And it was just he and I for quite a while, just working in the studio. I mean Don really helped me out at that point, he lent me money, that was a rough time right there for me.

"So anyways, Don and I just worked together. We weren't sure what it was going to be, I don't think we necessarily thought it was going to be Dokken. We didn't really know what it was going to be. So we were just writing. And then at one point Lynch Mob broke up so we contacted Mick and got him involved and he came out, early in '93."[201]

Inevitably, while working together, Don and Jeff spoke about some of the things that happened during their time in Dokken and some of the things that bothered Don.

---

201 Jeff Pilson interview with James Curl.

"When Jeff came back in '95 to work on my solo record, *Dysfunctional* which actually turned into a Dokken album, we got into conversations a couple of times time about what happened. When we would talk, I told him, 'Well, there are a couple of things you probably don't know, Jeff.' He said, 'What?' I told him, 'You know, you guys used to talk pretty loud when you were partying. Do you know what it's like to be the lead singer of a band and trying to get some sleep in your bunk when you have three guys up at the front of the bus plotting how to try and get rid of you?' It was like, 'Boy, if we could just get a better singer or a younger singer.' It was also stuff like, 'Jeff, you could do the lead vocals and we could go as a three piece if we could just get the name.' I had to listen to these types of conversations where people were just conspiring to try to undermine me. It didn't make me a real happy camper in the morning."[202]

After working together for about a about a year, fate unexpectedly stepped in when Ronnie James Dio came looking for a bass player. For Jeff, the chance to work with Dio was too good to turn down.

Explaining how these events unfolded, Jeff said, "It was sometime in the spring of 1993. I was milling around my house frustrated because my sprinklers were leaking and gushing all over the place and, being the least handy human being on the planet, I didn't have a clue what to do. Suddenly the doorbell rings, I go to answer and who is standing at my front door but Vinny Appice and Ronnie Dio. At that time I'd been friends with those guys for about 10 years, since Dokken's first tour with Dio at the end of 1983. I'd also been

---

202 Exclusive! Kirby's interview with vocalist Don Dokken, by Jeff Kirby, December 4, 2004

in a band with Vinny (War and Peace) and gotten pretty close to Ronnie as we both shared a love for Indian food.

"Anyway, after welcoming them and a few laughs, I asked them why the honor of the visit. They told me that they were in the process of reforming Dio (Ronnie and Vinny had reunited with Black Sabbath the previous year) and that Jimmy Bain was no longer going to be playing bass with them, so did I know of any bass players available? I immediately said yes, ME!!!!!! At that point I had been working with Don Dokken for a year writing and recording much of what was to be the 1995 Dokken album *Dysfunctional*. Mick Brown had recently teamed up with us, but it wasn't looking to be a full-blown Dokken reunion so my feelings were very mixed about it. The instant I thought about being in Dio, I was totally convinced it was the right move to make. Of course I had to break the news to Don, which wasn't fun at all. And I think he was quite upset with me, because I think he felt like I abandoned ship and I understand his perspective on that.

"Nearly every night of Dokken's touring with Dio during the '84 and '85 tour George and I would watch the band. They were such a force to be reckoned with, I just knew I had to be a part of it. So, immediately after saying yes, the guys said we should go jam, they had a rehearsal place right down the street. And it really was under two miles from my house to where they were rehearsing. But then I asked them, does anyone know anything about sprinklers? I already knew Vinny was one of the handiest guys around, and I soon found out Ronnie was pretty good at that as well.

"No sooner did I mention it before both of them jumped into action. They started running around my yard with a screwdriver and within minutes I had working and efficient sprinklers watering away. Off we headed to go make some music and begin the two month writing process for one of the most joyous album making experiences of my life with Dio's *Strange Highways*."[203]

After the release of *Strange Highways,* Jeff toured with Dio off and on for just over a year. Then in 1994 things began to heat up in the Dokken camp and a full-blown reunion was soon being discussed. With the *Dysfunctional* album nearly completed, Columbia wanted to get George back into the band. They knew that having the renowned axeman back would make the comeback legit, create fan interest and help drive album and ticket sales. Don, however, was initially apprehensive and didn't want to work with George, but the record label insisted on "the classic line-up."

John Kalodner, the legendary A&R executive who was in charge of negotiating the deal, spoke with Don and assured him that five years was a long time and people can change. Eventually, Don relented and got in touch with George. "He'd mellowed out and wasn't harboring any resentment," said George. "So I thought, okay."

Continuing on, George says, "Since I got back into it after the original relationship, the whole scenario had changed business-wise and in terms of the structuring of the band and I was left out of the loop intentionally. It was designed to keep me out. I was there as a figurehead. They needed my name to get signed and get the deals done and so forth, and to draw the fans in. But I was kept out of a lot of the business and the creating of the music, except for solos and stuff. It

---

203 Jeff Pilson interview with James Curl.

was pretty ridiculous. Basically they cut off their nose to spite their face."[204]

"Then it looked like George was going to come back and we were going to do Dokken, so then I left Dio," said Jeff. "It was late summer early fall of '94 that we decided that we would get back together, and that the first thing we were going to do was this acoustic thing which was great. That was Don's idea and I thought it was a brilliant idea; it was just a great way to come back. It was different, we could hear each other, the singing was really great and it was just a really nice way to reintroduce ourselves to each other. And that first night we did a show and we felt the chemistry together."[205]

Dokken's first come-back show was on December 12, 1994, at The Strand in Redondo Beach. The semi-acoustic set was filmed and later released on VHS, then on DVD. Despite the time apart, the guys performed together exceedingly well and decided to move forward.

With the success of the acoustic jam the guys got together and put the finishing touches on their come-back album, which was suitably named *Dysfunctional*. Available to the public on May 23, 1995 the LP sold well considering that bands like Dokken were still suffering from the crushing effects of grunge. *Dysfunctional* entered the charts at number 47 which was respectable for the time and sold just over 400,000 copies. However, sales slumped and it failed to hit the gold mark. It took some time, but the album eventually did achieve the USA RIAA gold certification a few years later.

---

204 Martin Popoff interview with George Lynch, October 18, 1999.
205 Jeff Pilson interview with James Curl.

Since eight years had passed from the release of *Back for the Attack*, the guys had matured and so had their writing. As a result, *Dysfunctional* is a departure from their hair metal past. Some of the songs carry a strong '60s influence coupled with a subtle serene neo-psychedelic style. While other songs branch out into a heavier blend of early '70s hard rock mixed with the progressive rock of the late '70s. And although the LP has many early influences, there is still just a dash of the '90s sound sprinkled into it—just enough to keep the sound modern.

For the most part the album is much more introspective and instrumentally diverse than anything Dokken had previously done. Because the album is so full of musical variety there are subtle things going on that often go unnoticed with just one listen. Many fans had to listen to it more than once to really gain an appreciation for it. For example the song "Sweet Chains," a slower, moody song with a hint of influence from the Doors, has a lot of nuances that are easily missed. Mick spent a considerable amount of time orchestrating all of the percussions on the song, utilizing an assortment of tambourines, shakers, bongos and bells.

Other outstanding tracks include "The Maze," "Too High to Fly," "Inside Looking Out," and "Nothing Left to Say." "Hole in my Head" with its great harmonies has a bit of a King's X sound and George does a nice job on the solo. The cover of Emerson, Lake and Palmer's "From the Beginning" is well done and adds a nice touch to the track list. "Shadows of Life" is another interesting piece with its doomy Black Sabbath like guitar sound.

Overall, *Dysfunctional* is an excellent album that is musically diverse but still manages to stay within the boundaries of classic rock 'n' roll. Unfortunately, the album went largely unnoticed during the reign of grunge, but just might be the best Dokken has ever done.

"For me," said Don, "*Dysfunctional* is the masterpiece. I really like it. Some people thought it was too Beatles-esque, and it had too many harmonies and it had this '60s thing going on, but I dug the album. And a lot of people did.[206]

"I love *Dysfunctional,* but George didn't have anything to do with *Dysfunctional*. His name is on one song. That was my next solo album, it was already done and finished. George came back in the band in the last week, he came back in and did a few solos and a couple of rhythms. But that album was done and wrapped up. It had some interesting things, the Beatles influence, the sitar [guitars], it wasn't just straight hard rock, it had some depth to it. It was a much deeper album and I had the luxury of spending eight months writing it, cause I owned my own recording studio so it wasn't like we were on the financial buck. It was my studio, my recording console and I could do what I wanted and take my time."[207]

"My memory of *Dysfunctional* is very positive," recalls Jeff. "I remember spending the better part of a year writing/recording/working with Don to get that going. A lot of good times in there. Having said that, I do think it would have been wise, after George signed on, to spend a bit of time writing with George to make it a little more "classic" sounding. But overall a solid record, IMHO - just not exactly a traditional Dokken record."[208]

---

206 Popoff Archive, 3: Hair Metal, Don Dokken, by Martin Popoff, Power Chord Press 2017.
207 Don Dokken interview with James Curl.
208 Jeff Pilson interview with James Curl.

Following the album's release Dokken began a run through the States playing mostly smaller venues. However, old hostilities began to resurface and things went downhill in a hurry. "Yeah, they did fairly quickly once we started touring," said Jeff. "George was definitely in a place where he was sabotaging a bit, I think. I think it was one of those things where he felt like he didn't want to see Don succeed, so he was willing to bring the whole thing down. He was very suspicious of Don's motives, he felt that he couldn't trust him and he couldn't know for sure that we were going to be an equal band again. And I think it made him feel sort of like despondent and he started sabotaging things; similar to how he had done on the Monsters of Rock tour. He kinda got into a similar head space although he was playing great and he didn't turn his back to the audience, but it got ugly.

"And we brought in a counselor to help us try and do our thing like Metallica did years later on in their movie. We tried to do that but it really didn't help because people weren't being all that forthright and honest with the guy. So we had the same old problems and there we were."[209]

By the time Dokken were on the Japanese leg of their tour, Don and George were barely on speaking terms. It was then that Don decided to confront the issue head-on.

"George was acting up on the *Dysfunctional* tour and I was like 'here we go again.' And he was nice for a month and he gets back in the band and he started right back up again. And I said, 'what is the fucking problem?' and I'll never forget we were in Japan, and he pointed up at our backdrop and said, 'that's the problem.' So, basically

---

209 Ibid.

because the band was called Dokken and he believed that I was getting all the kudos."[210]

Continuing on despite the growing difficulties, the guys began composing a new album in late '96 which would turn out to be the highly controversial *Shadowlife*. For the writing of the album Jeff, George and Mick collectively over-ruled Don and decided to update the sound of the band toward a more alternative style. This attempt to modernize Dokken's sound to what was hip at the time didn't sit well with Don, but he gave in nonetheless.

"Well, the change in sound was due to the fact that the world had changed so much and it was us trying to adapt plain and simple," said Jeff. "It was us trying to have a different approach—more modern or whatever. We had been listening to a lot of Tool records at that point. Plus, the producer, Kelly Gray, was very much from the whole Seattle world—not into the melodic rock world, really. Which kind of makes him an odd choice for Dokken, when you think about it.

"Once again, we were falling apart. Half the band was out in Phoenix, and I knew Don was unhappy during a lot of it. So it was just too spread out... It wasn't working well. So, how I look back on the record is that there were some nice moments, but overall it was just not an inspired piece of work. There's a couple of really wonderful things on there, but overall, not an inspired or a cohesive piece of work."[211]

Released on April 15, 1997 *Shadowlife* took unsuspecting Dokken fans by surprise with its grunge-like sound. Those who purchased the album were left scratching their heads

---

210 Ibid
211 *Blabbermouth*, Jeff Pilson talks Dokken turmoil, January 5, 2015.

wondering what happened to the band they had grown up with. Even to casual Dokken fans the change in sound was obvious. There are clear instances of Stone Temple Pilots, Tool and Soundgarden influences throughout. And it didn't work well, especially for a band known for its upbeat melodic rock, shredding guitar solos and big "power ballads."

Along with the shift to a '90s sound, several other things happened. George's famous guitar tone and soaring solos were all but gone. Instead, his guitar is much more down-tuned and the music in general is a lot more bass heavy. And while there are some decent solos on the album, most are lacking the firepower that made George one of the most influential players to come out of the '80s.

Also missing is Don's operatic singing and patented lyrics. Don's vocals are more subdued and on several tracks he uses vocal effects; like many of the newer grunge bands were doing. Overall, it's like the whole group was restrained and unalive.

However, there were a small percentage of fans that liked the album and appreciated that Dokken was not afraid to change direction and try something new. Yet for the hardcore fans there was little if anything that got them excited. There was nothing that gave them the feelings and emotions one gets from ballads like "Alone Again," or the raw energy from songs like "Into the Fire," "Lightning Strikes Again" or "Unchain the Night"—nothing that makes you pump your fist or bang your head.

Don's thoughts on the album. "It's a shit album, but I didn't care, I just didn't care anymore. I'm like, you guys want to do these songs? and they just basically said, 'we've decided these are the songs.' They gave me the music and I wrote the lyrics in about six days for the whole album. I just wrote bullshit, in my opinion the songs were bullshit. It wasn't Dokken. *Dysfunctional* sold 400,000. *Shadowlife* sold 50,000, the writing was on the wall. I had to explain that to them. I said, 'guys, we went from 400,000 to 50,000, there's a reason and don't tell me it's because of grunge, it has nothing to do with it.' It just wasn't a good record. But I was just tired of fighting. That's the way it was, basically it was a George Lynch, Jeff Pilson record.[212]

"I just don't like the album," said Don. "I don't mind the songs; I think that album would be a cool album if it was named something else other than Dokken. There are some cool cuts, if it were done by a band from Seattle. It just didn't represent Dokken. First of all, I didn't write any of the songs on the album, which I thought was kind of weird. I mean I wrote the lyrics and melodies, but I was removed from the project. George basically said flat-out that if you set foot in the studio, I'll leave the group. And I felt kind of silly. But that's how bad the relationship with George and I had become. I was excommunicated from the whole project.

"So I stepped into the album and just had to like, fit lyrics and melodies to existing tracks. So the concept was just a mess. Usually, you write lyrics and music that's supposed to fit to them. And when I got into the studio I said, 'Well, guys, right here there's seven bars of music, so can we just cut it out and get to the chase and go to the chorus?' And George would say, 'No, you're not cutting one bar out.' So I had to write more lyrics to add to the song, and I didn't have anything to say.

____

212 Don Dokken interview with James Curl.

"So, I found myself repeating myself lyrically just to fill in the holes. And to me that's just bullshit. So, I found myself being redundant, writing lyrics and making up bullshit that didn't really mean anything. So, I broke my own rule that I don't like to repeat myself and I don't like to write crap because I was forced into a situation that I swore I would never do. And I wrote four songs for the album and they were rejected by the guitar player. He refused to play any songs that were written by me. Because I guess before that the album was *Dysfunctional*, and all the songs were written by Jeff and I, and George didn't write any of those songs. So he was like, 'Well, you wrote everything on the last album, so I'm writing everything on this album.' It was silly."[213]

In support of the record the guys embarked on a tour with Alice Cooper, Slaughter and Warrant on August 2, 1997, but it was short lived. On August 22, after only playing half a dozen shows, the classic lineup came to an abrupt end with a physical confrontation between Don and George. Having had enough of each other, the two came to blows on the tour bus with George's son Sean having to break them up.

"I came on the bus late," said Don, "and George was in a hurry to get to the gym. I went to the fridge to get some orange juice and he came up behind me and started choking me. If you've seen George's muscles lately you know I didn't have a chance. Lucky for me George's son Sean pulled him off of me. I said, 'that's it.' I got my shit and went home. George had gotten into bodybuilding. I was finding needles on the bus, he was shooting up steroids. That was during his

---

213 Popoff Archive, 3: Hair Metal, Don Dokken, by Martin Popoff, Power Chord Press 2017.

steroid use days and he was having quote, unquote the infamous 'Roid Rage.' "[214]

Remembering the moment, Jeff remarked, "It ended on a horrible note. Don and George got into a bit of a fist fight on the last day of the Alice Cooper tour. And after that we got George to leave the band, because he was trying to demand more money. So we felt, 'ok, now we have to do what we can to survive.' And that's when we fired George and he got a lawsuit against us. We settled and we walked away with the name and he got a compensation package. So then we carried on and that's when we did the *Erase the Slate* record. It took us a while until we decided to get Reb Beach involved, but once we got Reb it was a whole other thing."[215]

Though many a fan considered *Shadowlife* to be Dokken's Funeral March and the departure of George the tragic end to a great band, there was still hope. And that hope came in the form of axe slinger extraordinaire Reb Beach and an album called *Erase the Slate*.

---

214 Don Dokken interview with James Curl.
215 Jeff Pilson interview with James Curl.

Chapter 12
Erase the Slate
and the Departure of Jeff

Having given George his walking papers, Don, Mick and Jeff began the hunt for a new guitarist. For a time John Norum stepped in playing a total of 15 shows, but because of prior obligations he was unable to stick around. Jon Levin, who would eventually become a permanent member, filled in for a time and played a dozen shows over the next several months. However, because he was a full time attorney, he was unable to commit to a permanent position in the band. It was then that the guys decided to bring Reb Beach into the Dokken line-up.

Richard Earl "Reb" Beach, Jr. was born August 31, 1961. As a young boy, Reb showed a propensity for music by playing the piano at four years old. His parents, excited at their son's apparent innate gift, believed he was a child prodigy. "I wasn't a child prodigy," said Reb. "I was just a guy with a good ear."[216]

Reb's mom eventually bought her son an acoustic guitar, which he promptly stuck under his bed and forgot about. "I wanted to be Billy Joel or Elton John, I thought I was going to be a piano player," said Reb. "Then I saw Kiss and that changed everything. I knew the instant I saw it; I knew that's what I'm gonna be."[217] From there it didn't take Reb long to blow the dust off his guitar and start building callouses on his fingers.

---

216 You Tube, Rock Scene, Reb Beach talks about his rock scene.
217 Ibid

Reb's early influences included many of the great '70s guitar players from bands like Boston, Aerosmith and the Outlaws. As a young boy, Reb would listen to these bands and pretend to be a rock star while playing his guitar on his bed, which served as a makeshift stage. By the time Reb was in high school he was known as skilled player and was voted most likely to become a "Rock Star."

For a young boy growing up in Pittsburgh there wasn't much of a music scene, but regardless Reb found a band to play in. In no time he and his bandmates became a popular act on the local backyard party circuit. "The band I had, we only knew six songs and we would play parties and sometimes we would play those six songs twice and that would be the set."[218]

As a young man, Reb eventually relocated to Florida and joined the band Fortune which played the Fort Lauderdale and Miami circuit for a number of years. After a falling out with the lead singer, who punched Reb in the face for quitting, Reb moved to New York where he got a job as a singing waiter. "And that was odd being a singing waiter, but I hung around at music stores— Manny's and Sam Ash."[219] Reflecting on the time, Reb said, "Pounding the pavement with two gig bags on my back in New York City was a great time in my life.[220]

"So, every day I would hang around and play guitar and talk to the guys who worked there. And I heard about an audition for Fiona. And I went there and there was like 20 guys—it was on Long Island. Anyway, all the guys at the

---

218 Ibid
219 Ibid
220 Ibid

audition were wearing spandex and their hair was all poofed out."[221] In contrast, Red was wearing blue jeans, a T-shirt and had long straight hair. "And I walked in and they said, 'you're hired,' without even hearing me play."[222]

Having landed the gig, Reb became a member of Fiona's backing band as well as an accomplished studio musician. Over the course of a couple of years Reb worked with the likes of Howard Jones, Chaka Khan, The Bee Gees, Twisted Sister, and Roger Daltrey, among others. Working with such renowned artists helped Reb establish a reputation as a musician who could adapt to various musical styles.

It was during his tenure with Fiona that Reb became acquainted with producer Beau Hill who introduced Reb to Kip Winger.

"So, I met Kip for the first time and we hated each other. Absolutely I thought he was so full of himself—absolutely conceited. You know he hated me and I hated him, but we did sessions together. And we started to get along a little bit better once we worked together."[223]

It was at this point that Beau suggested that Reb and Kip write together. "And I sat down to write with him," said Reb, "and that changed everything. I had this riff and it was the riff for 'Seventeen' and I didn't even know it was a song and I played it and he said, 'what's that?' And I said 'oh, it's just a riff that I play, sounds kinda like Ratt.' And he said, 'That's a song' and I'm like 'really?' So we wrote three songs in one day, 'Madelaine,' 'Time to Surrender' and 'Seventeen.' And I thought I had just met the greatest guy in the world and I

---

221 Ibid
222 Ibid
223 You Tube, Rock Scene, Reb Beach talks about his rock scene.

just wanted to hang around with him and learn from him. He taught me everything I know about song writing. And from then on we were pals and still to this day he's my best friend."[224]

From there the two aspiring musicians became roommates and eventually put the band Winger together in 1987. To handle the skins they brought in percussionist extraordinaire Rod Morgenstein, and the talented Paul Taylor to play keyboards and rhythm guitar. Together the quartet formed a well-rounded and capable band.

About a year later Winger released their self-titled debut album on August 10, 1988. The album was hugely successful, selling over 1,000,000 copies in America and from it came four hit singles: "Madelaine," "Seventeen," "Headed for a Heart Break" and "Hungry."

Following a successful outing with the Scorpions, Winger kept the momentum going with their follow-up album *In the Heart of the Young*. Much like their first album this one was massively successful and went one-and-a-half times platinum. Moreover, the record also produced three hits singles: "Can't Get Enuff," "Miles Away" and "Easy Come Easy Go."

Following the release, the boys headed out on a long winded 13 month world tour playing over 230 dates with the likes of Kiss, Scorpions, ZZ Top, Extreme and Slaughter. Worn out from life on the road, the guys returned home after the extended outing and took a well-deserved break. It was at this time that Paul left the band, citing exhaustion after years of constant touring.

---

224 Ibid

Along with all of their success, Winger quickly became regulars on MTV. It was during the mid-1990s that unfortunately they caught the attention of Mike Judge, the creator of the animated series Beavis and Butt-Head. On the show, Winger were often the subject of ridicule. Stewart, a neighborhood boy who was always trying to be accepted by Beavis and Butt-Head, was typically shown wearing a Winger T-shirt. This was in stark contrast to the AC/DC and Metallica shirts worn by the title characters. To Beavis and Butt-Head, the guys in Winger were uncool and a bunch of "wussies." Because of this the two often belittled their videos—particularly the "Seventeen" video. According to Mike Judge this was done because Kip Winger told MTV he would not let the show make fun of him.

In a 2005 interview, Reb said that this treatment on the Beavis and Butt-Head show caused a huge decline in popularity for Winger.

"So, we released the record (*Pull* in 1993) and went out on the road and that's when the floor fell out from under us practically overnight. Some guy came to the bus with a copy of *Beavis and Butt-head* and in it they hung a nerd up by his underwear while he wore his Winger T-shirt. They went to his house, and his loser family (including the dog) were all wearing Winger T-shirts. That week people stopped coming to our shows and record sales came to a screeching halt. 'Down Incognito' was taking off at radio when DJs just dropped it from their playlists because they were too embarrassed to have their station associated with it. A month later I called Atlantic Records and they had never heard of Winger."[225]

In his subsequent animated series *King of the Hill,* Mike Judge continued to poke fun at Winger. One of the show's characters John Redcorn, was a former roadie for the band until embarking on a Native American vision quest, where

---

225 Wikipedia, Winger

he found that, "Wrangling groupies for Winger was not my proper life path."

In a 2010 interview with Eddie Trunk on *That Metal Show*, Kip dismissed the rumor that he'd told MTV to not make fun of him. In an August 2011 interview with *Billboard*, Judge stated, "I thought Kip Winger had a problem with the show, but it turns out he was OK with it." Judge then explained, "We tried other bands' logos but nothing worked as well as the originals." [226]

With the constant bashing from Beavis and Butt-Head and the overall decline of hair metal, Winger disbanded in '94 with each member going on to various solo projects. Reb, who was basically broke at the time, borrowed some money from Kip and headed out to L.A. where he found a spot playing for Alice Cooper. Following a four-year stint with Alice, Reb decided it was time for a change.

"Well, I was playing with Alice Cooper at the time, and Kip Winger, who knows everyone, heard that Dokken was looking for someone. I got in touch with them, and we played together as an audition. I was fortunate that both Jeff and Mick liked Winger, so I had that going for me. It clicked right away, as I recall."[227]

With Reb in the band, the guys got busy writing a new album. For their new record they decided to return to form—trends be damned—and make a more traditional hard rocker. Their resulting effort which they titled *Erase the Slate*—a suitable moniker considering the *Shadowlife* disaster—turned out to be just that.

---

226 Ibid
227 Reb Beach interview with James Curl.

Giving his thoughts on the album, Reb said, "Love it!!! Dokken was starting to go with this dark '90s sound, and I think what we came up with took us back into the Dokken 'bang your head' thing that I always loved about the band. I love 'Lightning Strikes Again,' and 'Kiss of Death,' and I wanted something like that for the title track. *Erase the Slate* is a good Dokken record I think, because it has a lot of very solid riffs, songs, and hooks. Ninety percent of the songs are good songs, which is rare for a record. *Under Lock and Key* is still my favorite, though. George is a God. I am not worthy.

"Everything about it was great to begin with. Jeff and I turned out to be a great writing team, which is why I jumped at the chance to do the project I am doing with him now (the project that Reb is referring to is Black Swan). He has this positive energy that makes him great to write with for anybody, but we think alike, so it went quickly. I came up with riffs, and he wrote parts that tied it all together. It was very similar to me and Kip's writing process in Winger.

"There was a fantastic engineer on that record named Rob Easterday who was a big part of why it came out so well. It's funny, he talked about trains all the time, and played the video game 'Train Simulator' in his free time. He eventually became a train conductor in Pennsylvania, and goes through my town in Pittsburgh sometimes, driving a train with 100 cars.

"The first night Don came in to sing, he was two hours late. He came in with a bottle of wine and a very cute girl on his arm. Rob and I went into the control room, and he went into the vocal room that was separated from us by soundproof glass. We watched in shock as he made love to her on the table, and then they left."[228]

Remembering the moment with a laugh, Rob said, "He brought this young lady in and was out there with all these

---

228 Ibid

candles going. Don was definitely in lead singer mode that night. I was trying to engineer through the middle of it and get stuff recorded. That wasn't one of our more productive nights, you know, but what you gonna do?"[229]

The occasional distraction notwithstanding, *Erase the Slate* was released on June 15, 1999. For those Dokken fans who were leery after *Shadowlife* there was a collective sigh of relief. Right from the opening track ("Erase the Slate") the album was everything *Shadowlife* was not—it was alive! and upbeat! with scorching guitar solos and some of the best bass work Jeff has ever done. More importantly the guys apparently had a lot of fun recording it. And nowhere is this more evident than in the hard rockin' song "Crazy Mary Goes Round." The track features Mick on lead vocals and is a somewhat silly, raucous tune with an old-school vibe that highlights Mick's underrated chops and is guaranteed to get toes tapping.

"It was a fun rocker, it's just a fun old rock 'n' roll song," said Rob. "But it never clicked for Don and he was like, 'I'm just really not feeling this song.' So he or Jeff, one made the suggestion, 'Hey, Mick, why don't you sing it?' And it came to be. And of course Mick is such a ham and a great ball of fun, he had a great time. He stepped right in there and I don't think most people realize what an incredible vocalist Mick is."[230]

The album is also loaded with other outstanding tunes like "Maddest Hatter," "Change the World," "Voice of the Soul" and a very well done remake of "One" by Three Dog Night. And though the album does have a bit of the modern '90s sound mixed into some of the songs, it still offers up enough of the classic sound to keep most fans happy. In addition, Reb's faultless fret work is a pleasure to listen to and Jeff's bass solo on the track "Little Brown Pill" is just incredible.

---

229 Rob Easterday interview with James Curl.
230 Ibid

Overall, *Erase the Slate* is an underrated album that is a gem to discover. However, for the purists and diehard Lynch fans who say, No George Lynch, No Dokken! the album will probably never be accepted.

"As for *Erase the Slate*, I'm very proud of that record," said Jeff. "Considering how important George is to the chemistry, particularly with writing, I think we came up with a very solid Dokken record. Reb, of course, is a big reason. He's a brilliant player and writer and that made it happen. He's also got a great attitude, was open to suggestion and found a way to fit himself in, in a way that was natural and effective. It's funny cuz the actual process of working with Reb and George, for me, is not all that different. In both cases the egos go away and a collaborative feeling takes over. They're both brilliant, so for me I just listen and react, then if I have something to add they're very open. But both of them are an endless trove of great ideas. The individual quirks are different, but the workflow is strikingly similar."[231]

Though the album helped Dokken rebound from the *Shadowlife* debacle, it got very little fanfare and went largely unnoticed. The popularity of bands like Dokken was still at a low and album sales were way down. However, grunge, having reached its peak around '93 had out stayed its welcome and hair bands were starting to gain a bit of momentum.

Following the release of *Erase the Slate,* Dokken then put out *Live From the Sun*. This album captures Dokken at the Sun Theater in Anaheim, California, on November 4, 1999, playing through a live set of greatest hits and a couple from

---

231 Jeff Pilson interview with James Curl.

Erase the Slate. A video of the performance was also released both on VHS and DVD formats. Along with this live recording and *Erase the Slate,* Dokken finished out a very tough decade with aplomb and looked to forge ahead into the new millennium.

In 2001, Jeff became involved with the movie *Rock Star,* starring Mark Wahlberg and Jennifer Aniston. The movie tells the story of Chris "Izzy" Cole, a singer in a tribute band who becomes the lead vocalist in his favorite band Steel Dragon. The movie is of course inspired by the real life adventures of Tim "Ripper" Owens who was a singer in a Judas Priest tribute band. In 1996, Tim made headlines when he landed the gig to replace Rob Halford when Rob left Priest.

While in the band, Tim recorded two albums with his boyhood heroes. He was also nominated for a Grammy Award for Best Metal Performance in 1999, with the song "Bullet Train" from the album *Jugulator,* but lost out to Metallica's "Better than You."

For the movie, Jeff was hired to play Jorgen, the bassist in the fictitious band Steel Dragon while Zakk Wylde was Ghode, the guitarist, and Jason Bonham played the drummer known as A.C.

Speaking about his experience while making the movie Jeff remarked, "It was fabulous, it was so much fun. Tom Werman called me to play bass and originally I was brought in as a session bass player for the recordings because they did the music first. So, I came in thinking that's what I'm going to do.

"And we started rehearsing and Stephen Herek the director would come down to the rehearsals every day. And he watched the rehearsal and one day he just came up to me. And he loved the vibe that was going on in the rehearsal and I kinda became musical director as I tend to do in bands anyway. And so he liked the vibe and one day he came up to me and said, 'I love what's going on here, I want a band in this movie, I want it to be like a real band and you guys are. You're real musicians and you're interacting like a band. How would you like to be in the movie?' And I was like 'yes!'

"And it was just a great experience, it was a lot of fun. It was tedious work. Movies are a lot of sitting around and waiting. But everybody was great and we had a lot of laughs. From what I understand the actors were in a great place because it was a music movie and actors want to be musicians and musicians want to be actors. Everybody was fun, Mark Wahlberg, Jennifer Aniston all those people, really fun."[232]

During his involvement with the movie, Warner Brothers approached Jeff and Don with an offer for a record which ultimately led to Jeff stepping away from Dokken.

"I left in early 2001 right around when the *Rock Star* movie came out," explained Jeff. "The reason I left was because we had gotten an offer from Warner Brothers who was promoting the *Rock Star* movie. They were willing to put in more money in promotion for us than we had seen since the '80s for sure. But the tradeoff was we had to have a record done, set on a certain date when they were ready to go. And Don just wasn't ready to make that obligation. He said, 'We can't rush a record,' and I said, 'Well, no, but we can try and work really hard and take advantage of this opportunity.'

"He was right that you don't rush a record, but he was wrong because a lot of times he doesn't rush a record because he's lazy and other times it's just not worth the hassle; you can come to a resolution much easier. And I felt like to him

---

232 Jeff Pilson interview with James Curl.

it's more important about having control than it is the fortunes of the band. This was an opportunity we should not have missed. It was a big opportunity and we kinda blew that and I got very despondent and to me that was the final insult. I just couldn't understand that thinking at all. And that's when I said, 'I see where my future lies,' and I decided to leave."[233]

With Jeff out of the band, Don enlisted bassist Barry Sparks who had played in several outstanding bands such as: Yngwie Malmsteen, Michael Schenker, and UFO. From there Dokken marched on, touring steadily throughout 2001 and into 2002. It was at this point that Reb decided to move on from Dokken and join Whitesnake. However, it was with a heavy heart that he handed in his letter of resignation.

Remembering the time, Reb said, "Kip told me Whitesnake was looking for someone, so I sent them the *Live from the Sun* DVD, which was a good representation of my playing and my look at the time. I ended up getting Whitesnake, and the weird thing is that we (Dokken) were getting ready to open for Whitesnake! It was awkward when I had to call my friend Don and tell him that he was opening for me now. He was cool about it, though, and here I am 18 years later, and still in Whitesnake."

Continuing, Reb went on to explain, "I'd say being in Dokken was some of the best times I've had on the road. You could drink and do whatever drugs you wanted, providing you showed up and played your parts. We had parties on the bus afterwards every night. It was great being the guitarist. Maybe not the first show, because someone threw a Nike air pump hi top sneaker and hit me smack dab in the face, while people were screaming 'You suck!!!' and 'Where's George?' After a few shows it was heaven, though, because Don would sing two choruses and just let me play solos for as long as I wanted. The band started working out cool

---

233 Jeff Pilson interview with James Curl.

things, because as a three piece, you can just call out stuff on the fly. It was just me and Jeff on musical instruments, so we started to make up cool endings and breakdown sections. There were some great improv moments, which is harder to do when there are more musicians. Don was very kind to me on the road, and we have been friends ever since. I really love that guy."[234]

With Reb having bowed out, John Norum once again stepped into the Dokken mix and the guys began work on a new album.

---

234 Reb Beach interview with James Curl.

Chapter 13
Into the 2000s
and John Levin

Having lost Jeff and Reb certainly took a big toll on Dokken. However, with the capable Barry Sparks and John Norum in the band, the guys regrouped quickly and got busy working on a new record. A few months later they completed, *Long Way Home,* which was released April 23, 2002.

The album is an arrangement of up-tempo rockers with a few slower tracks mixed in. And although it's a solid composition, the mellower songs tend to bog it down somewhat. Because of this, the energy level isn't nearly as electric as it was on *Erase the Slate*. In addition, there is a sprinkling of "modern rock" production tricks done to help contemporize the music, which is unnecessary for a band like Dokken. That's not to say that the album is bad, in fact it contains several tracks that deserve a listen.

"Sunless Days," starts the album off nicely with a heavy Norum riff and some first-class fret work. "Everybody Needs (To be with Someone)," has a rocking '70s vibe, while "Under the Gun" cranks the tempo up to 11 and would have fit very nicely on *Tooth and Nail*. The groovy "Magic Road" is a catchy tune with a great guitar solo and "Heart Full of Soul," a Yardbirds cover, is well done.

The rest of the album, however is fairly tame. Don's love for the Beatles is unmistakable in the ballads "Little Girl," "Goodbye My Friend" and "I've Found." "There was a Time" is a nicely done poignant acoustic song that is worth a listen or two.

Overall, *Long Way Home* is a respectable album with moments of excellence and the occasional classic sound. Don's vocal performance and song writing are top-notch and the band plays well together. However, it could have used a couple more up-beat rockers to help ratchet up the energy, or perhaps less ballads.

Remembering his time in Dokken, John said, "In the beginning it was a lot of fun. I did *Up from the Ashes* in 1991. I stayed with them for about three years. We toured on that album like crazy; it was a lot of fun. Then, when Dokken reunited in 1997 I joined them once again, which was a lot of fun. I felt kind of silly sometimes ripping off George Lynch, but sometimes you just have to play what was written for the song. Then I did *Long Way Home* in 2001, and everything was totally changed, it was horrible. We did the album, and I went out with the band for one year, which felt like five years. Don used to be this cool person but he became this awful person that I didn't want to have anything to do with. He's got a lot of personal problems and it was just horrible."[235]

According to a source, John also had an issue with the tour and its accommodations, which were not up to the "rock star" standard to which he was accustomed. Being that bands like Dokken were still suffering from a huge drop in popularity, they were forced to adapt to a much different lifestyle than what they had enjoyed in their heyday. At this point Dokken was playing smaller venues, and making less money. As a result the five-star hotels were exchanged for

---

235 *Blabbermouth*, John Norum talks about playing with Dokken, upcoming Europe tour, September 17, 2006.

less expensive motels and the fine dining and limos were long gone. And apparently John wasn't happy.

No longer finding his spot in Dokken to be amiable, Norum departed during the Swedish leg of the tour they were on. To fill in, Alex De Rosso jumped in and stuck around for the remainder of the tour. Once back home in L.A., Don reached out to Jon Levin with the hopes that Jon would be able to join the band, despite being a full-time attorney.

Born March 18, 1966 in New York, Jon grew up in the '70s and '80s. Explaining how he got into music and came to join the band Jon said, "Dokken was my favorite band growing up. I was just a young kid in my teens in my bedroom playing to these songs. For me, for some reason, music came much easier to me in my head than anything else. I had trouble with school as a youngster. No one knew what attention deficit was back then. I couldn't pay attention long enough to read a page in a book at the time, you know. So for some reason, in my brain, music just took to me; it was easy for me.

"So when I was just a little kid, I mean very little, my parents were teaching me through lessons how to play piano. I was little, like three or four, probably four. I wasn't really good but I was able to learn. So I played piano for a couple of years. And then maybe when I was eight or nine they offered lessons in the school, so I started taking violin lessons.

"In fourth grade I found the trumpet and then I played trumpet for five years. I was actually a pretty good trumpet player, and the guitar I found when I was nine. And how I found guitar is, it was just an old nylon string acoustic guitar in our basement. And I saw that one day when I was going through the junk down there and I said, 'what's this?' And I just started playing it and I learned a few chords on my own and a friend of mine had an electric guitar with a little amp and the Beatles complete book and I go over there and I had never seen an electric guitar before. So at this point I'm probably 10. And I see the electric guitar and that just totally, I couldn't believe it, I was just blown away, you know with that book it showed you in tab how to play a chord. And I was learning how to play Beatles songs, basic little songs, "Eleanor Rigby," "Here Come the Sun." Then I took a couple of guitar lessons and I got a better acoustic guitar when I was 10 years old. I started getting good at that pretty quickly. Then I got an electric guitar when I was 11 and then when I was 13 I got a Les Paul, which I still have today.

"I went through phases with everybody. Eric Clapton, Jimi Hendrix, the Who, Zeppelin and then at some point somebody played "Eruption" for me and it just blew my head off. I didn't believe it was a guitar, I'm like 'it has to be some sort of a piano.' And once I hear that I was a huge Van Halen fan. Then I got into Lynyrd Skynyrd and Dokken for a long time.

"I dropped out of college to join a Long Island club band called Devias. And that's how it started for me, I was playing in the clubs in Long Island and Tommy Henriksen saw me play, then one day I got a call from producer Joey Balin asking if I wanted to come down and play with Doro Pesch of Warlock. So I met with Tommy and we went over the songs a bunch of times, and went down to SIR (studio), played and I got the gig. I was maybe 22 at that point. Then we did an album and toured and we did a headlining tour in

Europe, the Metal Hammer festival with Ozzy Osbourne and quite a number of shows.

"And that's how it started, and after that I got my own record deal with Tommy Henriksen and Bobby Rondinelli on Atlantic records, but that project really didn't go anywhere. Tommy ended up moving out to Los Angeles and he became friendly with Jeff Pilson and they were in a band called War & Peace together. About a year or two later I also moved to Los Angeles with a band I was in at the time looking to come out and get it going. Unfortunately, the grunge scene took over and once that happened I thought for me there was no future in pursuing a musical career. You know I'm a solo type of guitar player and there were no guitar solos anymore and once Nirvana hit there were no more guitar solos and I was like, 'oh, it's over.' Once that "Smells Like Teen Spirit" thing hit there were no more guitar solos. And then I ended up going to law school because I had to do something, because I thought my career in the music business was over.

"So I went to law school and my first year out of law school I started my own law practice. And I got a call to represent Jeff Pilson on a matter. So I was representing Jeff Pilson, then one night I got a phone call from Jeff asking if I could come down and play a couple of guitar solos for his band. But I had no idea it was for Dokken, I thought it was for one of Jeff's projects. I didn't even know Dokken was still playing or back together, I was out of the loop. I really didn't know what was going on. I was thinking it was for War & Peace or for one of Jeff's solo projects. My dad actually pushed me into to doing it, because I wasn't going to do it. I was actually in a suit and tie at my dad's house, cause I was gonna take him for dinner and it was raining. But he pushed me to do it. It was a rainy night, I drove down to Redondo Beach and when the studio door opened Don just handed a Les Paul to me. And I'm pretty sure he was pretty skeptical because Jeff probably said his lawyer's coming down to play. And they must have been like 'Are you fucking kidding me?'

"So he just hands me a Les Paul, he didn't even want to let me hear the music and he says, 'just play a solo' and I ask what key is it in and he says 'it's in E, just play a solo.' And I said, 'can I hear it?' and he said 'no, just play a solo.' I guess he just wanted to hurry it up and get me out of there. So I played two solos quickly, one on a song that was released called "The Irish Song" which was released on something in Japan. And then I played the first version of "Maddest Hatter" that sounds nothing like the latest version. I did solos on both of those two things and then a couple of weeks later Jeff called me and said, 'Hey, man, how do you do under pressure?' and I said 'why? What's up?' and he said we're headlining the Dallas Star Plex on July 4, can you learn the songs and do this gig? And I'm like 'Yeah, absolutely.'

"So he came over and we rehearsed a couple of times and we did a tune-up gig for Don's birthday which is June 29. So that was a few days before the July 4 thing and I drove down to Redondo Beach. Don gave me directions over the phone and he said we're playing at this place called, and what I thought he said was the Steak House, the Redondo Beach Steak House, and he told me where it was. Redondo Beach is somewhat tricky, I don't know my way around and I'm not from the South Bay and there was no navigation back then. And I remember going down there and driving around for two hours and I couldn't find the place, I was just gonna come home cause I was going to miss the gig. Time was going by, I said forget it, I was with my girlfriend at the time and I was just gonna blow it off and if I didn't find that something tells me that I would have never ended up in the band.

"And then at the last second she said, 'wait a second, look at all those people in that parking lot, is that it? The Stakeout?' It was called the Stakeout, not the Steak House! So I made it there by the skin of my teeth and we played that. Then we did the Star Plex on July 4, of '98, for like 20,000 people. And I hadn't been on a big stage for years at that point. So then I did about a dozen shows with Dokken. Then Reb ended up joining the band. I was a full-time lawyer and I think at the time Don made the right decision taking Reb. I had been out of the loop a long time. What was I gonna do, fold up my law practice? At that time it wasn't really going to be feasible regardless and Don took Reb and they did a record together. Then I think he had John Norum for a short time and then they had a fill in guy Alex De Rosso for a short time.

"Right around 2002, Don called me and asked me if there was a feasible way for me to really join the band, would it be possible and could it even work? And they were on tour with the Scorpions and he said, 'could you fly up here and come see the show we're playing in Vegas. And let's talk about how this could really work.'

"I went up there and we talked about it and I thought about it long and hard and realized maybe, because technology was starting to move along back then. Remember, things weren't like they are today, how the internet is, you know it was very different, phones were different, computers were different. So I devised a way that I could plug my cell phone into my laptop and make it act in such a way that you could get email. So I was able to devise a way that I could work from the back of the bus. I bought a fax machine, a laptop and this device that you could plug the phone in. So that's how I did it. And I joined the band, we wrote a record and I worked from the back of the tour bus for years."[236]

With Jon finally a permanent member of the Dokken mix, the guys turned their attention to putting together the album *Hell to Pay.*

Released on July 13, 2004 the album turned out to be a solid effort with some rockin' tracks and superb axe-work by Levin. In fact, he was praised by hardcore Dokken fans for his Lynch-influenced style of play. "Escape," "The Last Goodbye," and the speed metal track "Don't Bring Me Down" are good, but the two tracks that really shine are "Haunted" and "Better Off Before."

Yet even with these outstanding songs the album is dragged down a bit by a couple of songs that are entrenched in the '90s and early 2000s sound. Moreover, one gets the impression when listening to the LP that the band is holding back and not unleashing the metal beast within.

In general, *Hell to Pay* is a good album, just not the album Dokken needed to reestablish their melodic metal dominance. Thankfully, that would all change with their follow-up release *Lightning Strikes Again,* a splendid album that would recapture the classic Dokken sound and take the listener on a trip back to the '80s!

---

236 Jon Levin interview with James Curl.

Chapter 14
Lightning Strikes Again
and Broken Bones

Having had a couple of good but not great albums, it was high time for Dokken to release something exceptional.

"It's time that a band from our era did something special and proved that our brand of music is still valid," said Don. "Our goal was to create an album that was our best since our heyday."

To prepare for the writing of the album and get his head in the right place, Jon made a CD of his favorite Dokken tunes and gave it to Don. For months, while writing the new album, Don immersed himself in old Dokken tunes, some of which he hadn't listened to for years. In the end, influence paid off.

Speaking of composing the album Don said, "It was difficult to write this CD, I am older and see the world through different eyes. Yes, it was a trip back in time, but I knew this is what the fans wanted, so we gave it to them.[237]

"Yes, it was very difficult. It's hard to go back and write an album when you're 30 years old and I am over 50. So, yes, I had to get back in that mindset. This is what the fans wanted, and if I stay focused on that I would give them a straight-ahead Dokken album.

"I personally like to put the Beatles influence in like on *Long Way Home* and *Dysfunctional*. I like those albums. I am proud of those records. I understand like Jon said, 'We

---

237 Don Dokken Exclusive Collider Interview, by Steve "Frost" Weintraub, May 2008.

are Cheerios, people like Cheerios and they want to eat Cheerios. If you give them Cheerios with salsa flavoring, they won't like it.' So we just wanted Dokken. This is straight Cheerios no salsa. So I took the salsa out, which was the Beatles influence and this album is very straight-ahead Dokken."[238]

"I had been sort of bugging Don," remarked Jon, "to try and do something that was, you know a little bit like keeping with the original sound. In the past we had the discussion and he kept telling me, 'You know it's hard for me as a writer, you're talking about stuff I did over 30 years ago. I don't remember the frame of mind I was in.' And I said to him, 'You know what? Look, I'll make a compilation CD, I'll burn one for you and you can put it in your car and start listening to the old stuff to get into the right frame of mind.' At the time I had all these riffs that were not the same riffs as the old songs but reminiscent you know, because I was into that style back then. You know I was a huge Dokken and George Lynch fan and I had all these riffs that I thought would really work well with the band.

"So, after he rolled around in his car with those tracks and then when we would write together he got back into it, you know, and we were able to do something that in my opinion sounded like a Dokken record without ripping off what they did in the past; it just sounded like a good next step. I was really happy with that record."[239]

Between August of 2007 and January of 2008 the guys were busy recording *Lightning Strikes Again* at Total Access

---

238 *Blabbermouth.net,* Dokken front man says Levin is 'more talented' than George Lynch, August 1, 2008.
239 Jon Levin interview with James Curl.

recording studio in Redondo Beach. With the album wrapped up in late January, Dokken headed out in early February for a show with Poison and then a one-off with Queensrÿche. However, Don wasn't doing well. After years of taking painkillers, due to the beating he took in Hawaii, his health both physically and mentally had deteriorated.

"It was, you know '91 when I got hurt. Guy tried to kill me in Hawaii, which started it all," explained Don. "Guy clubbed me in the hotel room, like a baby fucking seal. And he attacked me, and almost killed me. That's what started the whole painkillers, Vicodin, and then OxyContin. Next thing you know it's Morphine and Demerol, and is just a slippery slope. I could function like Keith Richards—he keeps going. But it was killing me spiritually and mentally, and I get tired all the time, and I'm drinking on top of it, and taking sleeping pills to go to sleep. I'm a Heath Ledger here if I don't stop. I've had a couple of close calls with almost choking, and on the Queensrÿche tour I was bloated and my voice was shot, and I was tired, depressed, fucked up on Morphine, and I'm just, you know, I was out of it. Drinking Jack, and I just came home and said, it's over. I'm going to Dr. Drew. That's when I went. I saw that on TV, I saw that guy in the wheelchair, Jeff from Taxi, (the TV show) and I thought, that's me.

"And that's when I started on the painkillers. And that started a slippery slope. And it took 15 years to graduate to heavy doses of painkillers, because you get immune to them, you know? It's not pretty, trust me. If I knew what I was going to go through in rehab, I wouldn't have gone. I was fuckin' hallucinating, freaking out, seizures, I was a mess. They underestimated my addiction, and I just, I don't remember much. I just remember being in Las Encinas

Hospital, and in my room, and the next thing I know, I woke up after 36 hours and I was in a lockdown psych ward. And I said, 'What happened?' And they said, 'You snapped. You were swatting at cobwebs and you were crawling around on the floor.' And I'm like, 'I was? What happened?' 'Well, we underestimated your detox protocol, so you went through like a heroin withdrawals.' And your brain just shuts off and protects itself. Because your body is screaming for its drugs, and I went through withdrawals and I just snapped. So I'm clean now. It was great. I'm over it. There's a story. And I was in there, and told myself, well, quit smoking, quit drinking, quit everything. I'm already here (laughs).

"I was in there for three weeks, hanging out with Steve-O (from the movie Jack Ass). He owns it. He told me, 'I'm going to rehab!' So it was just him and I going to our little drug counseling every day. So I didn't know. I honestly didn't know. A lot of people know. You should go to a psych hospital or rehab, some of these people are drug seekers. They're on the street scoring, trying to get high, doing anything to get drugs. That was never me. I didn't take drugs to get high. I could say that. I did it because I am in pain. I've tried other things. I've talked to a million specialists and they all told me the same thing, 'Take this pill.' And then you take stronger and stronger and stronger doses, and then you're on fucking Morphine, which is glorified heroin, and you're hooked, and you can't get off of it. You can't. You had to go into the hospital and detox, otherwise you have a heart attack. It wasn't pretty. But it was interesting.

"So, life is good, and like I told the band, I'm not sure I remember the last couple of tours we did. I was kind of in a fucking heroin Jack Daniels haze all the time, and nobody ever knew it. It's like Alice Cooper always said, 'I was a total alcoholic, throwing up blood,' and nobody remembers Alice being like that. And Alice was the first one to say, 'Dude, I was chugging a fifth of vodka and nobody knew.' He was straight as an arrow. And I was the same way. No one saw me falling down drunk. I'm not that kind of guy. I don't get falling down drunk. And nobody knew I was fucking up on opiates. They're not all jacked up on Morphine. Well, the Queensrÿche guys kind of knew, because I slept all day long (laughs). And they would wake me up, 'Uh, Don, you go on stage in an hour, you want to wake up?' Yeah, so I wake up and do a show, and go right back to my bunk. I was overmedicated. I was really overmedicated. And I didn't realize it until I was talking to Eddie and Geoff, and they said, 'We're really worried about you, man. You sleep all day and you don't look good and you look like you are not feeling good,' and I'm going, 'Well, I'm hungover and I'm fucking medicated to the teeth, and I'm overmedicated, and I just got a call home.' So, I literally came home for a day. I hopped in my car and said, 'Dr. Drew? I saw him on TV' and said 'I'm going there' (laughs). I hopped in my car and just drove myself there at midnight, middle of the night, and said, 'I'm going to check in. I need help.' Checked myself in for three weeks."[240]

Following his three-week stint in Las Encinas, Don regrouped with his bandmates and Dokken readied themselves for the release of *Lightning Strikes Again*.

On April 8, 2008 fans were treated to the new Dokken release, and what a treat it was. The album entered the Billboard Top 200 at No. 133, the band's highest chart

---

240 Martin Popoff interview with Don Dokken.

performance since 2004 and was praised as the best Dokken record since the band's classic era.

The album starts off with three outstanding songs that have the classic Dokken sound, "Standing on the Outside," "Give Me a Reason," and "Heart of Stone." All three are melodic, guitar oriented songs that are reminiscent of the '80s and have a very *Under Lock and Key* feel. Jon's nimble fingered fret work, not only on these songs but throughout the entire album is exceptional. Moreover, he is able to effectively emulate an inimitable Lynch-like style while retaining enough of his own musical personality to keep his playing original and fresh.

In addition the album features plenty of great vocal harmonies and melodies, which is done especially well on "Heart of Stone." And though Don may not be able to hit those high notes like he did in the 80s, his voice which is a little grittier than it was in his youth fits the overall feel of the songs.

Following the first three tracks the album takes a decidedly slower turn with "Disease," which was originally written by Mick and was hit and miss with many fans. It's a bass heavy track reminiscent of the down tuned '90s sound and Don uses heavy vocal effects. Though not a bad tune, it doesn't fit well on an album that strives to deliver a melodic based '80s sound.

"'Disease,' that one didn't sound like the other songs," mused Jon. "That was something Don had from earlier that he really wanted to finish, so I just worked with him on it and changed a few things. I really like that song. Don wanted to have a couple that were different, he didn't want every song to be a reminiscent song. It's a good song, it's just a different head trip."[241]

"How I Miss Your Smile," a ballad, and "Oasis," a mid-tempo tune, keep the momentum mellowed, but they can't keep it contained. "Point of No Return" cranks things back up to 11 with a near Speed Metal like pace, a scorching solo and an overall *Tooth and Nail* like feel.

From there the album takes another slow turn with "I Remember," the best ballad on the LP, and then steps back on the gas with the hard hitting "Judgement Day." The energy slows once again with "It Means" and the quasi-ballad "Release Me." However, the album finishes up strongly with "This Fire," an absolute ass-kicking track in the vain of "Lightning Strikes Again" with an old-school riff and an air-guitar worthy solo that shows just how good Levin is.

Having captured their fans' attention with *LSA,* Dokken headed out on tour in July for a two-month trek across the U.S. with fellow Sunset Strip band Poison and former Skid Row singer Sebastian Bach.

During the tour, Barry and Mick were not part of the line-up. Mick had signed on to play with Ted Nugent for the summer before Dokken was offered the slot on the Poison tour. Meanwhile, Barry was in Asia performing with a stadium act. To take Barry's place, Chris McCarvill from House of Lords jumped aboard and Jeff Martin of Badlands fame played drums for a short while until he was fired by Don. Chris McCarvill's House of Lords' bandmate B.J. Zampa was then brought in as drummer for the rest of the tour.

---

241 Jon Levin interview with James Curl.

Having finished up their summer schedule, Dokken continued playing shows for the remainder of the year with a variety of bands like Great White, Bonfire and Kingdom Come. It was around this time that Chris left the band and Sean McNabb was hired as the new bassist.

On November 29, 2009 during an encore at a Dokken show at The House of Blues in Anaheim, George, Jeff and Mick joined Don on stage for two songs. It was the first time that the quartet had played together in 12 years. This one-off reunion show sparked all kinds of talk not only among fans but the band as well. In early 2010, Lynch announced a reunion of Dokken's "classic" line-up on his website, however the announcement was quickly followed by a retraction on February 24.

Three months later, in May of 2010, Don and George were guests on *That Metal Show* (Season 5, Episode 7) with Eddie Trunk and were expected to announce a reunion. However, things didn't turn out as planned and the reunion was a bust. As a result both guys were angry at each other and verbal barbs were hurled during interviews which were later posted on various websites.

"There was a lot of talk about a Dokken reunion," explained Don. "I tried my best to make it happen for the fans with Jon's blessing. But the bottom line was Jeff said he was busy with Foreigner for the next few years, so that was that. When I agreed to do *That Metal Show* we were going to announce a reunion but at the last minute Jeff asked me not to talk about it because he had not mentioned it to Mick Jones yet. I totally understand, just wish he would have said something before I agreed to go on the show with George."[242]

Giving his thoughts on Don and the failed reunion during an interview with Guitar International's Rob Cavoto, George said, "I feel like a fool because I got played again for the last fucking time! Like an idiot I went along with it but looking back I see what he was really doing. He was blowing wind in his sails by creating the impression that there was a reunion pending. That people were going to wake up and pay attention, that his guarantees were going to go up, and people are going to show up to his shows thinking I'm in the band. If we did reunite we would be working for him. He's a miserable guy and he will stay miserable in his own skin. I wouldn't want to have 100 million dollars and live in that guy's brain. He's just a piece of shit."[243]

By the end of the year it looked as if a reunion of the glory days' line-up might never happen. On December 8, 2010, Lynch announced on his website that a Dokken reunion would not be happening saying that, "We feel it's important to let folks know there will be no Dokken reunion in the foreseeable future, if ever. This is Don's decision, despite Jeff's and my best intentions and efforts over the past few years to make this happen in good faith. My apologies to VH1, Eddie Trunk, Steve Strange and all the fans who were pulling for this to happen."[244]

With talks of a resurrection of the classic line-up having fizzled out, Don and Mick refocused their attention on Dokken. Jeff continued on with Foreigner and George kept

---

242 *BraveWords*, Don Dokken: There was a lot of talk about a Dokken reunion; I tried my best to make it happen, May 19, 2011.
243 George Lynch on Don Dokken: He is just a piece of shit. May 20, 2011.
244 Wikipedia, Dokken.

himself busy for the next few years touring with Soules of We and Lynch Mob while doing various side projects. One such project was T&N, (short for Tooth and Nail) a band put together by George, Mick and Jeff that featured a collaboration with several different singers including: Tim Ripper Owens, Sebastian Bach, Robert Mason and Doug Pinnick. Together they put out the album *Slave to the Empire,* a collection of well-done Dokken covers mixed with a number of originals. George, Jeff and Mick would later be involved in another "Super Group" with Robert Mason called The End Machine, which released its self-titled debut album in 2019.

It was in 2010 that the opportunity to do something unusual was offered to Dokken—a TV commercial for Norton Internet Security 2011, at the time the latest virus spyware and internet protection. Don was offered the spot by his director friend Ryan Ebner, however after hearing that the commercial involved a dead chicken, Don was a little apprehensive.

"I said, 'Yeah, I'll do a commercial.' He's, like, 'It'll be you and the chicken.' And I went, 'No, no, no, no, no, no. I'm not gonna punk myself.' And then he told me how much he'd pay me. And I went, 'Really?' He goes, 'Dude, it's Norton Antivirus.' I said, 'For that kind of money, I'll wear a chicken suit. I will be the chicken. I will flap my wings and I will cluck.' "

The commercial starts inside a colossal hangar that once housed blimps during World War II. With the guys staring down angrily at a whole raw chicken on a table a serious voice breaks in with the following funny narrative. "Imagine this chicken is your hard drive and the '80s metal band

Dokken is a computer virus. Dokken does not like chicken and wants to destroy it. The chicken, not knowing Dokken's intentions, doesn't really have any feelings either way. Now you have a choice. Would you like to allow Dokken to have its way with your chicken, unleashing a wrath the likes of which the chicken has never seen? Or would you like to deny it?" The guys then collectively do a pelvic thrust and the chicken blows up in flames and smoke. The voice then returns to say, "Protect your chicken from Dokken, deny digital dangers with Norton Internet Security 2011."

Regarding how he and his bandmates came to be featured in the commercial, Don told *The Classic Metal Show*, "It just fell in my lap. That was totally a fluke. We were on the road. Where I live, I have two houses on my property, and one of them is like a crash house for directors and producers and stuff; I rent it out. And one of the directors was gonna do this commercial, and it was supposed to be with Styx. And apparently, at the last minute Styx pulled out and they [the directors] were at a crunch, and I just happened to be home pulling in the driveway coming off one of our shows. And at this company he works for—HSI Productions—they do all these commercials and stuff—he said, 'Hey, I'm staying at Don Dokken's place and I think he's home; I saw his car in the driveway.' They asked me if I wanted to do it, and I said, 'When are you filming? We're kind of busy.' They said, 'On a Monday.' And this was, like, on a Thursday. And I said, 'Yeah, I'm off Monday. We leave Tuesday to go back on the road.'

"So we just whipped in there... I said, 'What do you want me to do? I mean, we can't prepare...' He goes, 'You just need to... It's just a dead chicken...' (laughs) I didn't have a clue. I go, 'What do you mean a chicken? A chicken chicken? A live chicken?' And he goes, 'No, it's a dead chicken, and you're a virus. It's a metaphorical commercial.' I said, 'Hey, I don't care. That's fine.' So I went down and did it. And they pay ungodly amounts of money and you just stand there and look mad at a chicken. And I guess there's three different versions of the commercial; there's one where we're eating the chicken, and you have the pelvic thrust ending where it explodes; and you have the one where it pulls a switchblade and tries to shank me and I say, 'Bro, this isn't over yet.' "[245]

By 2012 it was time for the guys to once again get an album out. However, at this time both Don and Jon were going through problems with their health. In early 2012 Don was diagnosed with stomach cancer and Jon was having problems with his left hand. During an interview on *The Classic Metal Show* Don went into detail about the ordeal saying, "I had a tumor, ya know I had cancer and that was a little bit of an eye opener and luckily I beat it. But I was pretty sick doing *Broken Bones*, I didn't do chemo, but I did radiation and it kicked the shit out of me. I wasn't healthy, I put on 35 pounds and was bloated from radiation and my voice sounded like crap. Ya know I thought that I was toast.

"And just when I started getting better Jon's left hand went to sleep, he couldn't feel his hand, he couldn't feel his fingers. And I'm like, 'What the fuck's going on, Jon?' And he had to go to a specialist. So they took out a rib and they cut into his neck near his carotid artery, it was a very dangerous surgery. And then they had to go in and they cut him and cut all his muscle tissue because he had some very

---

245 *Blabbermouth,* Dokken Frontman talks about chicken commercial, Lynch Mob tour rumors, September 15, 2009

rare genetic thing where he had two extra ribs. And so he couldn't play and I'm like, 'Great, you can't play, I can't sing, we're fucked! But we still cranked out *Broken Bones*.

"But it was kinda like, 'When you're feeling good, Jon, come on over and we'll work.' And then sometimes he would be feeling up to playing after the surgery and I just had a radiation dose and I'm like, 'I'm in no mood to sit here and help you and produce your guitar tracks. All I want to do is go to sleep.'

"You know it got so bad that in the middle of that whole thing, I had to take a pee and my bathroom was five feet from my bed and I would sit there and ponder over it for about an hour, 'Can I walk that far and walk back to the bed? I don't know. I think I'll just hold it a little longer.' I mean I had no energy, zero. I was slamming Red Bulls, coffee, anything I could do to try and keep my spirits up. So I told my doctor, 'Man, I'm really depressed with my career, I don't know what's going to happen, you know I need some medicine, some anti-depressants,' and my doctor goes, 'Don, you need a dog.' And I said, 'What kind of doctor are you? I just want a happy pill, just give me a pill to make me happy.' And he goes, 'You need a dog.' "

Taking his doctor's advice, Don got a dog… and, "I got Cody, and Cody is the bomb, and I love that dog. It forced me to get up and take him for a walk and go up in the mountains and take him for hikes, take him out to go to the bathroom. So he helped me get my spirits up and then I got well and Jon got well."

With Don and Jon having recovered, the guys finished up *Broken Bones*. Don though felt that the time had come to stop making records and decided that this would be Dokken's last.

"We spent 11 months on this record," said Don. "This is our last Dokken record. I'm not doing anymore Dokken records. So I said, 'Jon, I want this to be our swan song and I want to make a statement and I want it to be as good or better than *Tooth and Nail* and *Under Lock and Key* which is an impossible task but we're gonna give it our best shot.'"

Their resulting effort, *Broken Bones,* may not be as good as *Tooth and Nail* or *Under Lock and Key* but it's certainly a fine follow-up to *Lightning Strikes Again.* And although it just missed being as good as its predecessor—it wasn't by much. Furthermore, it may well be the single greatest gem in the Dokken catalogue. For this album Mick was away touring with Ted Nugent, so Don brought in session drummer Jimmy DeGrasso. This marked the first Dokken album that Mick didn't play on since the classic line-up had formed.

Broken Bones hit the public on September 25, 2012 and was well-received by the majority of fans. The album is a departure from *LSA* in that it is an evolution of the band musically. Most notably the album is moodier and the production is heavier when compared to the more polished and lighter sounding *Lightning Strikes Again.*

Another notable change on the record is Don's vocals. After having surgery to remove nodes in late 2010, his voice is in better shape, being less gritty and a bit smother. Unfortunately, Don can no longer hit notes in the higher register, but the music is accordingly tuned to accommodate this and doesn't detract from the overall quality of the record. As for the songs, there are a number of good ones. "Empire," "Best of Me," "Blind," "Broken Bones" and "Burning Tears" are real standouts. And for those fans who love great guitar work there are plenty of catchy riffs and high-voltage solos.

And like he did on *LSA*, Jon proves he deserves to be placed among the great axe slingers of the '80s.

As a whole, *Broken Bones* is an excellent album that gets better with every listen. The one knock fans had was that it's somewhat formulaic with several of the tracks sounding too similar, while others complained that the album sagged in the middle because of the slower ballads. Guess you can't please everyone.

"I like *Broken Bones,* it's my personal favorite," says Jon. "I just thought it was the next step for us while still sounding sort of like a Dokken record, but a little bit evolving. And I thought there was just some great songs on it like "Burning Tears." I like seven of the songs on that record that I think are just really good. At the time I had a surgery, Don had a surgery and we couldn't tour and we wanted to wait putting that one out but we couldn't convince the people to wait on it, so unfortunately it came out without our ability to tour it. So the album went unnoticed. And honestly it took the wind out of my sails. I was so pleased with that record and then after that I really felt like I didn't want to do another record. I got bummed. You know we spent so much time on it. Some of the sounds are just killer and I was pleased with the guitar parts and I just liked most of it. We spent like a year and a half making that record. Imagine you spend that kind of time on something and it comes and goes, it's disheartening."[246]

"Yeah, if you listen to it once you won't grasp the gravity of what we're trying to accomplish," explains Don. "The second time you realize that all of these songs are kind of different and they have their own flavor and their own vibe, their own groove. It's not just nine songs, the same old thing.

---

246 Jon Levin interview with James Curl.

I really worked hard. Jon and I spent 11 months and wrote over 30 songs. Some of these we rewrote three and four and five times. I really pushed myself on this one. It's our last CD so I said, 'This has to be it. I want everything to be stellar'"[247]

However, the lack of sales and fan response was disappointing to Don. The lead singer expressed his feelings during an interview saying, "I worked so hard on that record for months and months and months. I was disappointed. I thought it was a very strong record. The European label didn't really do anything. They just kinda threw it out there, and that was it. I went, 'Wow, what a waste of work.' It's not the money thing for me. I don't need the money. It's just, I love to make music. I like to write, and I like to put my thoughts and ideas to music. If I can't get those thoughts out to fans, it's disappointing."[248]

For the next three years, Dokken kept up a consistent tour schedule playing festivals and even making an occasional foray overseas to places like Germany, Brazil and Sweden. By 2015, rumors of a Dokken reunion once again began to swirl around the rock 'n' roll community and this time there would be no stopping it.

---

247 *Blabbermouth.net*, Don Dokken: Why Broken Bones is final Dokken album, October 5, 2012.
248 Ibid

Chapter 15
The Big Reunion

As early as August of 2015 rumors of a Dokken reunion were spreading quickly. In an interview with *Glide* magazine George spoke about the possibility of the band playing together again saying, "That comes and goes every couple of years, so who knows. But we are talking again about that."

Several months later it started to look as if a full-fledged reunion would indeed happen. However, Don was a little leery as everything hadn't been ironed out, despite the fact that George, Jeff and Mick had already leaked some of the details.

Don, who wasn't happy about his bandmates' loose lips, admonished the other members for jumping the gun before the particulars of the band's reunion were made official. "Mick said we were doing it a month ago, George has been saying it, and Jeff was saying it," said Don. "Which I have to laugh, because I said, 'Please don't anybody talk about it until the contracts are signed,' and I hadn't signed the contracts until a couple of days ago."[249]

Continuing, Don went on to say, "Doing a tour like this is not easy; there's a lot of logistics, money, accountants, taxes, overhead, equipment, video. It's a lot of logistics to put together, and it's taken a long, long time to put this Japanese tour together. But we did it, and we're gonna do six shows.

"Everybody was talking like it was a done deal, which is a very bad thing to do. You should never announce a tour before it's announced, because then the promoters think we're gonna do it no matter what, and it kind of hurts my

---

249 *Blabbermouth*, classic lineup of Dokken announces "Unleashed in the East" tour dates, August 3, 2016.

negotiating skills. If we say we're gonna do this, and we're kind of bartering about how much money, and they feel we're gonna do it no matter what—if it's a half a million or million dollars—I said, 'Please don't say we're doing it, because it hurts my negotiating position.'"[250]

By early August of 2016 Dokken officially announced that they would indeed be getting back together, for the "Return To The East Tour." However, their outing would be short—only one date in America and six shows in Japan.

Explaining how the guys were finally able to pull off a full-fledged reunion, Jeff said, "It came about because of Tom Mayhue who works for Gun N' Roses. Tom was in talks with Creative Man, a booking agency in Japan and they made us an offer and they made us a really good offer. They actually got a copy of the Foreigner itinerary and booked the shows around the time I had off because they wanted it to happen so bad. It was kind of a no brainer, you know they made us an offer we couldn't refuse."

When asked about the reunion George said, "It's like getting back together with an ex-spouse."[251] The guitarist then went on to say, "Well, um, it's a mixed bag. It's complicated. But the overarching feeling I have is I'm glad it's happening for the right reasons. One of which is money. But another of which is putting a nice bow and closure on an important part of our professional and artistic lives, and also for people who care about this kind of music. Because it was important to *their* lives. And with all the bad things going around it's nice to see that people can come together sometimes. I just think it makes people feel good. I know it's a drop in the bucket, but, you know, I'll take it." [252]

---

250 Ibid.
251 Dokken's George Lynch on the band's "complicated" reunion, by Richard Bienstock (Classic Rock)
252 *Classic Rock*, Interview Dokken's George Lynch on the band's "complicated" reunion.

Don, giving his thoughts on the reunion, had this to say: "I am very excited to come back to Japan and play with the members of Dokken that I spent so much time with. Being that it's only six shows, we are going to make it as spectacular as possible."

Continuing on, Don explained during an interview with *The Classic Metal Show* how the reunion came to fruition. "Years and years ago, I made a comment offhandedly, like, 'You wanna do a reunion tour? I'll do it for this amount of money.' It was like a one and a lot of zeros. And that was my price, and everybody said, 'You're crazy.' And I said, 'Well, that's my price, and I'm not gonna do it for anything less.' And now, fifteen years later, somebody came up with that price.

"So I approached George and Jeff, and I said, 'You guys wanna make a shitload of money for about one week of work?' And I told them the price, and I told them how much I wanted and how much they'd make, and, basically, they could make more money in one week than they'd probably make in several years. And so everybody said, 'Okay.' So I said, 'Well, I'll do it on the condition that I don't wanna do it in America or Europe or anywhere else; just six shows in Japan.' Cause we were very big in Japan, and it's just a… It's a reunion tour. So they agreed."[253]

Continuing, Don said, "This is a chance for redemption. We're trying to keep it positive. We're older and mellower now. We've been talking on the phone back and forth – 'How about this? What songs do we want to play? What song do you want to start with?' Dokken was not really a band that spent our weekends barbecuing together. That's not a negative; that just wasn't the way it was. There was so much

---

253 Don Dokken interview on *The Classic Metal Show*, 2016.

unfortunate mud-slinging when we broke up, which happens with so many bands but we're more legendary for it. So we're all trying to keep a positive attitude. As Jeff put it, 'I've always felt we never got a chance to put the exclamation point on the career of our lineup.' So this will be it."

And finally Mick, who had his trepidations about the reunion said, "Nothing's changed. I know George and Don, during the conversations to get this going, they're already starting up. And Jeff and I are kind of… Jeff seems excited about it.

"I would like to see it happen with nothing… There's not much time, so I know we've just gotta get in and do it and go, and Jeff will then get back to Foreigner, 'cause they barely give him any time off; he's only got a ten or twelve-day window, I guess, to do this. So we don't have any time for much bickering. But I'm a little standoffish about it. Maybe I'll get a good feeling from it when it happens; I hope to."

Continuing, Mick went on to say, "Listen, I hate to say this… I would love to do it for all artistic reasons and I'd really like to be excited and go, 'Oh, the band's back together.' But I don't feel that way. And I've gotta be honest with you. I just don't. It's a money thing, and the money's too good. Listen, I'm tired of the bad-attitude stuff. And you put Don and George together, and it just starts happening again, and then it gets really confusing. I think it's very sad when grown men act that way. And I'm tired of being around it, but here we go. And listen, for that kind of money, I'll shut up and do what we used to do. Jeff and I will stand there and go… just the same way we did before. Right now, it seems like it's only gonna be about six shows, I think, and if we blink, this will be over."

Mick went on to add, "You know, what's probably gonna happen is we'll probably end up doing it, it'll come off really well, really successful, and then they're gonna talk about doing it again. And I'll be, like, 'Oh, man. Here we go, all over again.' (*Laughs*)"[254]

The tour began on September 30 at Badlands Pawn, Gold & Jewelry concert hall in Sioux Falls, South Dakota, which was basically a warm-up gig following a couple of days of rehearsal and radio interviews.

From there the boys headed to Japan where they played their first show on October 5, at Namba Hatch Osaka, followed by shows at Fukuoka Civic Hall on the 6th, Tokyo on the 8th, Hiroshima on the 10th, Aichi on the 11th and finally back to Tokyo on the 12th for the final show.

While in Japan the guys filmed a DVD titled: *Return to the East Live 2016* that captures the band's live performances. In addition there is a lot of behind the scenes bonus footage as well.

Back home Dokken put the finishing touches on a new song and video, "It's Another Day," which was released on *Return to the East Live 2016,* in April of 2018. The song does a good job of capturing the classic Dokken sound and George delivers a simply amazing guitar solo.

"George and I came up with a couple musical ideas," mused Don, "and we sent it off to Mick, who wrote some lyrics," Dokken says. "I've got some lyrics. Jeff's home (from Foreigner) for a couple days this week and has a studio in his house. So we're gonna go to Jeff's and brainstorm and come up with a collaborative effort. We just thought it would be kind of cool to throw in a brand new song and make it interesting."[255]

---

254 *Blabbermouth,* Mick Brown says that Don Dokken and George Lynch 'are already starting up' with their bickering, August 23, 2016.
255 *Billboard,* Dokken frontman talks reunion concert, new song and more, by Gar Graff, August 31, 2016.

When asked about putting the new song together Jeff said, "It was great, it was just natural. The original plan was to try and come up with a new song before we went to Japan, and we were going to record it live on stage. We had talked about that before, but that doesn't always work out (Laughs). That is actually not the best situation for recording a new song, but what did happen was George and I got together, wrote the music for it, we were quite happy, gave it to the other guys and they liked it.

"We didn't start working on it until we got back from Japan, but as soon as we did that, Don made some suggestions, he suggested we speed the song up. We did and we all liked that. The vocals then got nailed quickly. It was just one of the more painless Dokken recordings ever, which is great because it came out so fabulous. It was just a real positive experience."[256]

Speaking of the DVD, Don remarked, "After 25 years, it was great to reunite with George and Jeff and Mick and do a couple shows for the fans. We hope you like this album and video. There's a lot of great bonus footage of us having fun, so enjoy it."

Jeff added, "I'm so thrilled this piece of the Dokken story is hitting the streets. What a magical experience it has been and this CD/DVD captures a lot of that wonderful manic energy that has always made Dokken so vital! I remain extremely grateful to have been a part of such a vibrant voice in the world of heavy rock. Thanks to the fans and to George, Don and Mick for being the musicians, writers and friends that you are!"[257]

---

256 *Cryptic Rock*, Jeff Pilson talks Dokken, Foreigner and life in rock 'n' roll, April 10, 2018.
257 *Billboard*, Dokken frontman talks reunion concert, new song and more, by Gar Graff, August 31, 2016.

Sometime later, during an interview, Jeff commented on the reunion saying, "I think we were all a little bit tense about it ahead of time—we didn't know what it was gonna be like. But once we got all the negotiations out of the way and we got to play together and started playing, it was actually really great and it was a wonderful experience. We got to kind of be friends for a while, which was really cool. I mean, I do a lot of stuff with George and I see him frequently anyway, but it was really cool… And then we did a new song that came out amazing. And then we did a couple of remakes of old songs acoustically that came out amazing. So it was really a positive experience. The tour was really fun. All the stuff we did with recording was really fun. It was a much more positive experience than we were expecting, and I'm really proud of the record; it did quite well. And it's pretty special that I got to experience that.

"Maybe there will be some more somewhere down the line; you never know. It's really hard to deal with the schedules that we all have. But if that was the last thing we ever do, it was a really great way to go out."[258]

With the success of the reunion there was a lot of interest from promotors to try and keep the Dokken momentum going. Yet, despite the repeated offers to book the band, Don was adamant that the Japanese dates were the only shows the group was going to do.

"Of course, everybody came out of the woodwork," remarked Don. "And they want us to do Sweden Rock, Wacken festivals, M3… People are throwing money at us to do a Dokken reunion in the States and Europe, and my answer to everybody is, 'No. It's not gonna happen.'

---

258 *Blabbermouth.net,* Jeff Pilson on Dokken's 2016 reunion. 'It was a much more positive experience than we were expecting,' July 9, 2018.

"I feel bad for my agents, 'cause they're getting bombarded from these offers for us to play these big festivals all over the world as a reunion, but I'm just not interested; I'm sorry, I'm just not." Continuing, Don stated, "Jeff's busy. He plays like crazy in Foreigner. He's on the road. George is out, you know, playing the bars with Lynch Mob, so everybody's busy. So I don't see any reason… I can't say, 'we can make all this tons of money…' And we're doing this tour for a lot of money, but I'm doing it to put an exclamation point on a very temporary reunion."[259]

Moreover, Don said that the reason there are no plans for the reunited Dokken to carry on is the fact that the current lineup of Dokken—which includes Mick, longtime guitarist Jon Levin and bassist Chris McCarvil—is still very much an active entity, with a consistently steady schedule of live shows booked throughout the year.

Speaking of Dokken's current lineup, Don said, "I'm so happy with Jon Levin and Chris. I mean, we get along so, so good. We're happy. We get on a plane, we fly to a venue, we hang out together and we go to dinner and we do the show and we hang out in the dressing room. It's very easy; you know, there's no drama. And at my age now, the last thing I need in my life is drama.

"I love the band I have now; we've been together for 13 years, and I don't want to hurt that franchise. Plus, if we were to continue with the original lineup, old wounds might be opened, and I don't want to revisit that. I don't think any of us wants to. It's all great when a marriage fails and you say, 'I'm gonna get back with my ex'—for a week, maybe. Six months into it, the wounds come back. I don't want to experience that. It's just not part of my life anymore, and I

---

259 *Blabbermouth*, Classic lineup of Dokken announces only U.S. tour date, August 9, 2016.

think the other guys feel the same way. So this will be enough."

Jeff, sharing his thoughts on the tour and how things turned out, said, "We weren't our best on that tour by any means, but the cool thing for me is we actually got along pretty good. It wasn't bad. The vibe was not bad and there were some moments of real laughter and fun. And I would rather be in a situation like that in that band, rather than be amazingly great but not getting along. I'm too old to have that ugly vibe anymore. But we had fun. Like I said, it wasn't our best performance although I think we cobbled together a pretty good live record. And the cool thing is we went in and we wrote a new song and collaborated on the track and it came out incredible and it's very Dokken like and it was probably one of the most painless recordings we ever made. So there was definitely a pot of gold at the end of that rainbow. There's probably not going to be a whole lot more on that, but if that's the last shows we ever did together, I think we ended up on a positive note and I can feel good about that."[260]

With the reunion completed, the guys headed back to their respective bands and picked up where they'd left off. For the fans, especially in America, the short tour was disappointing and left everyone clamoring for more. Nevertheless, for Don, George, Jeff and Mick the reunion was a nice way to end things and they parted as friends. And regardless what the future holds for Dokken they will always be connected by the incredible music that they created together; music that helped define the '80s and a unique era of rock 'n' roll history.

---

260 Jeff Pilson interview with James Curl.

As for us fans, we will have to be satisfied with the great catalog of songs that Dokken has left us. To be certain they gave us a memorable gift of music that should be cherished and enjoyed.

Jeff Pilson and James Curl, NAAM 2019.

Wendell Neeley and James Curl
Heavy Metal Hall of Fame 2020.

It's a little blurry but here it is, James Curl and Don Dokken, Heavy Metal Hall of Fame Induction, 2020.

Dokken Album Discography

Breaking the Chains, 1983
Tooth and Nail, 1984
Under Lock and Key, 1985
Back for the Attack, 1987
Dysfunctional, 1995
Shadowlife, 1997
Erase the Slate, 1999
Long Way Home, 2002
Hell to Pay, 2004
Lightning Strikes Again, 2008
Broken Bones, 2012

Live Albums

Beast from the East, 1988
One Live Night, 1996
Live from the Sun, 2000
Japan Live '95
From Conception Live: 1981, 2007
Return to the East Live (2016), 2018

Compilation Albums

The Best of Dokken, 1994
The Very Best of Dokken, 1999
Change the World: An Introduction, 2004
The Definitive Rock Collection, 2006
Greatest Hits, 2010, *An Introduction to Dokken,* 2010

Extended Plays

Back in the Streets, 1979

Singles

Year	Single	Peak positions			Album
		US [6]	US Main [7]	UK [4]	
1979	"Hard Rock Woman"	—	—	—	Non-album single
1981	"Young Girls"	—	—	—	*Breaking the Chains*
	"I Can't See You"	—	—	—	
1982	"We're Illegal"	—	—	—	
1983	"Breaking the Chains"	—	32	—	

Year	Title				Album
1984	"Into the Fire"	—	21	—	*Tooth and Nail*
	"Alone Again"	64	20	—	
	"Just Got Lucky"	—	27	—	
1985	"The Hunter"	—	25	—	*Under Lock and Key*
	"In My Dreams"	77	24	—	
	"It's Not Love"	—	—	—	
	"Unchain The Night"	—	—	—	
	"Will The Sun Rise"	—	—	—	
1987	"Dream Warriors"	—	22	—	*Back for the Attack*
	"Burning Like a Flame"	72	20	78	

Year	Single				Album
	"Heaven Sent"	—	—	—	
	"Prisoner"	—	37	—	
	"So Many Tears"	—	—	—	
1988	"Walk Away"	—	48	—	Beast from the East
	"Alone Again (Live)"	—	—	—	
1995	"Too High to Fly"	—	29	—	Dysfunctional
	"Shadows Of Life"	—	—	—	
1996	"From The Beginning (Live)"	—	—	—	One Live Night
1997	"Puppet On A String"	—	—	—	Shadowlife
	"I Feel"	—	—	—	

Year	Single				Album
1999	"Erase The Slate"	—	—	—	*Erase The Slate*
	"Maddest Hatter"	—	—	—	
2002	"Sunless Days"	—	—	—	*Long Way Home*
2004	"Escape"	—	—	—	*Hell to Pay*
	"Better Off Before"	—	—	—	
2008	"Standing On The Outside"	—	—	—	*Lightning Strikes Again*
2010	"Almost Over"	—	—	—	*Greatest Hits*
2012	"Empire"	—	—	—	*Broken Bones*
2018	"It's Another Day"	—	—	—	*Return To The East Live (2016)*

"—" denotes releases that did not chart